# RUSSIAN BATTLESHIP
## VS
# JAPANESE BATTLESHIP

## Yellow Sea 1904–05

ROBERT FORCZYK

Osprey Publishing,
Midland House, West Way, Botley, Oxford, OX2 0PH, UK
44-02 23rd St, Suite 219, Long Island City, NY 11101, USA
E-mail: info@ospreypublishing.com

A CIP catalog record for this book is available from the British Library

Print ISBN: 978 1 84603 330 8
PDF e-book ISBN: 978 1 84603 863 1

Page layout by: Ken Vail Graphic Design, Cambridge, UK
Index by Alison Worthington
Typeset in ITC Conduit and Adobe Garamond
Maps by Bounford.com, Cambridge, UK
Bird's-eye-view maps by Ian Palmer
Originated by PDQ Digital Media Solutions
Printed in China through Bookbuilders

09  10 11  12  13    11  10 9  8  7  6  5  4  3  2

FOR A CATALOG OF ALL BOOKS PUBLISHED BY OSPREY
MILITARY AND AVIATION PLEASE CONTACT:

Osprey Direct, c/o Random House Distribution Center,
400 Hahn Road, Westminster, MD 21157
Email: uscustomerservice@ospreypublishing.com

Osprey Direct, The Book Service Ltd, Distribution Centre,
Colchester Road, Frating Green, Colchester, Essex, CO7 7DW
E-mail: customerservice@ospreypublishing.com

www.ospreypublishing.com

**Acknowledgements**

I wish to thank Kendra Slaughter at the Boston Museum of
Fine Arts (MFA), Sabine Skae at the Vickers Photographic
Archive, Dmitry Malkov and the staff at the US Navy
Historical Center in the Washington Navy Yard.

**Dedication**

This volume is dedicated to 1LT Matthew C. Ferrara,
2nd Battalion, 503rd Airborne Infantry Regiment,
173rd Airborne Brigade Combat Team, KIA near Aranus,
Afghanistan on November 9 2007.

**Artist's note**

Readers may care to note that the original paintings from
which the battlescene plates in this book were prepared
are available for private sale. All reproduction copyright
whatsoever is retained by the Publishers. All inquiries
should be addressed to:

H. Gerrard
11 Oaks Road
Tenterden
Kent
TN30 6RD

The Publishers regret that they can enter into no
correspondence upon this matter.

**Editor's note**

The following will help in converting measurements referred
to in the text between imperial and metric:
1 mile = 1.6km
1lb = 0.45kg
1 yard = 0.9m
1ft = 0.3m
1in = 2.54cm/25.4mm

# CONTENTS

# INTRODUCTION

*If new warships are considered necessary we must, at any cost, build them… At present, Japan must keep calm and sit tight, so as to lull suspicions nurtured against her; during this time the foundation of national power must be consolidated; and we must watch and wait for the opportunity in the Orient that will surely come one day. When this day arrives, Japan will decide her own fate…*

Count Hayashi Tadasu,
Japanese ambassador to St Petersburg, 1895

When Japan emerged from more than two centuries of self-imposed isolation as a result of the Imperial Meiji Restoration in 1869, its political leaders rapidly set about developing military capabilities that would enable it to fend off foreign threats and pursue an independent foreign policy. The Imperial Japanese Navy (IJN) was established in the same year, with a hodgepodge of minor warships but a zest for modernization and self-improvement. Japan's new government turned to Britain – the acknowledged naval superpower of the day – to assist it in developing a modern navy. Despite the lack of a domestic heavy industrial base or significant amounts of foreign capital, Japan embarked upon an ambitious program to build a modern fleet that would be capable of defeating either the Chinese Navy or foreign squadrons in the region. However, Japan initially lacked the resources to purchase capital ships from the West and when China bought two 12-in gun battleships from Germany in 1885, this forced the Japanese naval leadership to revise their plans. It was not until 1893 that Japan had the financial resources to order its first modern battleships, the *Fuji* and *Yashima*, from Britain. Yet these battleships were not available when the Sino-Japanese War erupted in 1894, forcing the IJN to fight China's battleships with only its squadron of cruisers. Its victory in the Sino-Japanese War removed China from the balance of naval power

in the region and provided combat experience for the new IJN. Furthermore, as part of the Treaty of Shimonoseki that ended the war, Japan acquired the Liaodung Peninsula, including the valuable naval base at Port Arthur.

While Japan was beginning to modernize, Imperial Russia was expanding its sphere of influence out to the Pacific coast by moving into the vacuum created by the crumbling Manchu Empire. Vladivostok was acquired from China in 1860 and upgraded to a naval base in 1871. Initially, Russia had great difficulty exerting influence in the Far East due to the distances involved, but in 1891 construction began on the Trans-Siberian Railroad to link Moscow with Vladivostok. When it was learned that Japan would acquire Port Arthur, Tsar Nicholas II enlisted diplomatic support from France and Germany to block Japan's triumph. The so-called Triple Intervention on April 20, 1895 threatened Japan with war with all three European powers unless it abandoned its claim to Port Arthur. To back up his threat, the Tsar ordered the battleship *Imperator Nikolai I* to steam toward the port of Nagasaki. Lacking battleships,

Japan could not risk a naval confrontation with the European powers and was forced to evacuate Port Arthur. Eight months later, Japan's leaders had to meekly watch as the Russian Pacific Squadron appeared in Port Arthur and secured a 25-year lease on the port. By 1898, the Russians had reinforced their squadron in Port Arthur with the arrival of the battleships *Navarin* and *Sissoi Veliki*.

This diplomatic humiliation at the hands of Russia created a strong desire in Japan for revenge and a realization that further Japanese expansion in Asia would likely result in war with one or more European powers. Despite limited financial resources, a new ideology known as *Gashin Shōtan* ("Persevering through Hardship") led to increased budgets for the IJN. Rear Adm Yamamoto Gombei, from Japan's Navy Ministry, drew up a plan for a "Six-Six Fleet" based upon six battleships and six armored cruisers – a fleet powerful enough to defend Japanese interests in the event of war with Russia. Yamamoto managed to get ¥138.7 million (£13.8 million) from Chinese war reparations earmarked for new naval construction. In 1896, Japan's legislature approved the "Six-Six" program as the Ten Year Naval Expansion Program, authorizing the purchase of four more battleships from Britain. Together with the two *Fuji*-class battleships completed in 1897, Japan expected to have six modern battleships ready before it made its next move in mainland Asia.

In order to consolidate its sphere of influence in the Far East, Russia began assembling a modern battle fleet at Port Arthur, beginning with the battleship *Petropavlovsk* in May 1900 and soon followed by three more. By the end of 1903, the Port Arthur squadron consisted of three battleships of the *Petropavlovsk*-class, two of the *Peresviet*-class, the *Retvisan* and *Tsesarevich*, as well as seven cruisers and

China's acquisition of two battleships armed with 12-in guns from Germany in 1885 upset the naval balance in north-east Asia and spurred Japan to purchase battleships from England. When the Sino-Japanese War began in 1894, the Japanese Navy had only cruisers to fight these two formidable Chinese battleships. (Naval Historical Center, NH74378)

25 destroyers. During the same period, the IJN created a fleet based at Sasebo consisting of six battleships, 10 cruisers and 40 destroyers, poised to duel with their Russian opposite numbers for control of the Yellow Sea and the Tsushima Strait. In order for Japan to deploy ground forces into Korea, it would be necessary for its navy to control these bodies of water, and prevent Russian naval interference with Japanese landings. The stage for war was set when Russia refused to honor its promise to withdraw from Manchuria, and Japan severed diplomatic relations on February 6, 1904.

Navies were in a period of flux during 1888–1905, as the first modern battleships emerged to replace the previous generation of coastal defense monitors and masted turret ships. New technologies in naval gunnery, armor plate, fire control, explosives, communications and engineering plants were emerging at a rapid rate and navies had to build and deploy warships with untried sub-systems. Both Japan and Russia based their naval power upon battleships, usually armed with 12-in guns, which were mainly based upon British and French technology. Both sides had to make difficult decisions in preparing their battle fleets for war and in a period of sweeping technological change it was easy to make mistakes that could prove costly on the battlefield. Japan and Russia each made choices, some faulty, that combined to produce the battleships that fought for naval supremacy in 1904–05. At great cost to each nation, two great fleets were assembled – one based at Port Arthur, the other at Sasebo – set to battle for control over the Yellow Sea when the Russo-Japanese War broke out in February 1904. This duel for maritime power, fought between battleships of roughly equal force, was the first and last pure duel between battleships before submarines and airpower arrived to change the calculus of naval power.

The pride of the Japanese fleet had yet to sail. The *Mikasa*, fitting out in an English dry-dock in 1902. Ordered in 1896 to a modified *Majestic*-class design, the *Mikasa* cost ¥8.8 million (£880,000) and would serve as Togo's flagship for the duration of the Russo-Japanese War. (Naval Historical Center, NH58982)

# CHRONOLOGY

**1869**

Imperial Japanese Navy (IJN) is established after Meiji Restoration.

**1882–86**

Introduction of quick-firing (QF) naval guns.

**1888**

First coincidence rangefinder made by Barr & Stroud.

**1888**

Britain develops Lyddite explosive.

**1889**
July

Britain begins building *Royal Sovereign*-class, setting the standard for pre-dreadnought battleships.
British develop Cordite propellant.

**1891–93**

Harvey armor developed by American engineers.

**1892**

Japan develops *Shimosa* explosive. Franco-Russian treaty of alliance drafted.

**1894**

Britain begins building *Majestic*-class battleships.

**1896**

Krupp armor developed in Germany.

**1897**
August 17

*Fuji* commissioned, first Japanese battleship.

**1898**
January 8

Russian Naval Ministry orders concentration of 10 battleships in Pacific under "For the Needs of the Far East Program."

March 27

Russians acquire 25-year lease on Port Arthur.
Telescopic sights begin to be introduced on 6-inch guns.

The Tsar sent the battleships *Sissoi Veliki* (front) and *Navarin* (back) to form the nucleus of a battle squadron in Port Arthur in 1898. In 1902, they returned to St Petersburg as the Naval Ministry decided to send its newest battleships to the Far East. (Naval Historical Center, NH84771)

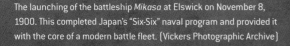

The launching of the battleship *Mikasa* at Elswick on November 8, 1900. This completed Japan's "Six-Six" naval program and provided it with the core of a modern battle fleet. (Vickers Photographic Archive)

The battleship *Hatsuse* was sunk by two Russian mines on May 15, 1904, along with the *Yashima*. After this catastrophe, Togo was more cautious with his four remaining battleships, which influenced his tactics at Yellow Sea. (Naval Historical Center, NH58971)

## 1899

**August 1**     Russian *Petropavlovsk*-class battleships begin entering service. Marconi wireless sets begin installation on capital ships. Royal Navy attempts first long-range gunnery exercise (5,500 meters).

## 1901

Improved FA2 rangefinder introduced in Britain.

## 1902

**January 30**     Anglo-Japanese alliance.

**July 24**     Captain Rozhestvensky's gunnery demonstration at Reval (Tallinn) impresses the Tsar and the Kaiser.

## 1903

FA3 rangefinder introduced by Barr & Stroud, for use up to 7,300 meters.

## 1904

Armor Piercing Capped (APC) projectiles introduced.

**February 9**     Battle of Port Arthur.

**April 13**     Battleship *Petropavlovsk* sunk by mine.

**May 16**     Japanese battleships *Hatsuse* and *Yashima* sunk by mines.

**June 20**     Tsar Nicholas II decides to send Baltic Fleet battleships to reinforce Port Arthur squadron.

**August 10**     Battle of the Yellow Sea

**October 15**     2nd Pacific Squadron under Admiral Rozhestvensky leaves Reval.

## 1905

**May 27**     Battle of Tsushima.

# DESIGN AND DEVELOPMENT

## NAVAL DEVELOPMENTS, 1860–96

After centuries of relatively slow progress, naval warfare underwent a radical transformation in the mid-19th century. In 1860, France commissioned the *Gloire*, the first steam-powered ironclad warship, followed 14 months later by Britain's *Warrior*. The *Gloire* and *Warrior* pointed the direction toward a blend of the latest developments in hull forms, armor plate, heavy guns and advanced steam engine plants that promised to yield a powerful new type of capital ship. By 1873, Britain had built HMS *Devastation*, the first sea-going turret ship, setting the broad outline for future battleships. However, the path toward developing the battleship from these early ironclad prototypes proved difficult. Western navies groped uncertainly toward integrating these new technologies into a practical warship design; constrained by limited budgets, but enjoined to develop prototypes quickly to avoid falling behind the efforts of other navies. It took another 29 years of trial and error before modern big-gun, ocean-going battleships became a practical reality in 1889–92. Britain's *Admiral*-class, begun in 1880, refined the features of the modern battleship with breech-loading 12-in guns and a secondary armament of 6-in guns. When Britain began constructing the *Royal Sovereign*-class battleships in 1889, the standard for naval power was set for a generation.

As the battleship concept evolved between 1873 and 1895, there were three key design issues that had to be answered in order to perfect the battleship into a combat-worthy weapons system. First, what was the best solution for firepower – turrets or barbettes, how many guns of each caliber and what type of ammunition? Second, what was the best scheme for distributing armor plate to achieve maximum protection of vital spaces? Third, what was the best means of achieving maximum speed and range?

The earliest ironclads had a limited number of large, slow-firing guns and no secondary armament. Early turrets were extremely heavy and forced ship designers to place them as low in the hull as possible to avoid instability – which resulted in low freeboard and poor seaworthiness. Barbettes, with the main guns rotating on a platform inside fixed armor, were considerably lighter and could be placed higher in the hull – resulting in better freeboard and seaworthiness. Britain leaned toward barbettes after several accidents with turret ships, but France doggedly pursued the perfection of the turret.

Initially, naval artillery firing cast-iron round shot from smoothbore cannons had difficulty penetrating even a few layers of wrought-iron armor plate, but in 1863 an elongated iron projectile known as "Palliser" shot was developed in Britain, which could penetrate up to 10ins or more of wrought-iron armor plate. Although the development of compound steel armor in the 1870s redressed some of the vulnerability caused by armor-piercing shells, it also spurred the development of bigger naval guns with better shells. Naval artillery was revolutionized in 1885, when Britain introduced the breech-loading 12-in/25-cal gun with improved muzzle velocity, and France introduced "Holtzer" steel projectiles that could penetrate compound steel armor. Furthermore, French scientists developed a powerful new explosive known as "Melinite" and a smokeless propellant known as "Poudre B." Britain purchased the patent for Melinite and dubbed it "Lyddite," and improved upon Poudre B with its own propellant known as "Cordite," introduced in 1889. When these new technologies were combined, they resulted in steel armor-piercing shells, equipped with much more powerful burster charges and propelled at much higher velocity, which made naval combat far more lethal than it had been previously. The only remaining problem was that large-caliber guns of this era fired less than one round per minute, which meant that an enemy warship might be able to close and inflict serious damage, as occurred with the Austrian ramming attacks at the Battle of Lissa in 1866.

The development of armament on battleships was also influenced by the nature of threats and by the expected range of naval combat. A general fixation on ramming attacks from other battleships gripped most European navies up to the late 1880s and spurred the requirement to add secondary batteries with higher rates of fire to battleships. Between 1884 and 1888, the British firms Elswick and Vickers and the French firm Schneider began perfecting new types of "quick-firing" medium-caliber naval guns that could engage targets with a high volume of fire, thereby discouraging ramming attacks. These designs were perfected by 1892, with the introduction of the Elswick 6-in/40-cal QF gun and the Canét 6-in/45-cal M1892, which could fire 5–7rpm using fixed ammunition. By the early 1890s, most navies had settled on the 12-in/40-cal gun as the optimal main armament, supported by a secondary battery of 6-in QF guns. While the maximum range of a 12-in/40-cal gun was over 13km, the lack of rangefinders and the

The battleship *Sissoi Veliki* in 1897. This was the first modern battleship designed for the Russian Navy, incorporating Harvey armor, 12-in/40-cal guns and Belleville boilers. (Naval Historical Center, NH84780)

use of simple sights made gunnery duels beyond 5km impractical. Indeed, in the early 1890s, gunnery experiments by the Royal Navy indicated that main guns could achieve only 30 percent hits at a range of 1.4km. Combat results from the Spanish-American War in 1898 appeared even less promising, where American warships firing at ranges of only 1.1–4.5km achieved 0–5 percent hits with 12-in guns, 5–9 percent with 8-in and 1–3 percent with 6-in guns. Thus, the lesson absorbed by the men who designed the battleships used in the Russo-Japanese War was that a battleship had little chance of knocking out its opponent strictly with main gun fire and would have to "slug it out" at close range with all its weapons.

A further complication in designing battleship armament was posed by the emergence of the torpedo threat. In 1870, the British engineer Robert Whitehead perfected a compressed-air powered torpedo and tests revealed that a single torpedo hit could inflict crippling damage on a battleship that had not been designed with underwater protection in mind. The Whitehead torpedo had a range of less than 1km and it was slower than a maneuvering battleship, but it was inexpensive and could be mounted on very small warships. In short order, Whitehead marketed his design to France, Germany and Russia, which began developing small torpedo boats to deliver the new weapon. Given the low rates of fire and poor accuracy from battleship main armament in the early 1880s, it seemed possible that large numbers of small torpedo boats could get in close enough to sink a battleship. In France, the *Jeune École* began trumpeting the torpedo boat as an inexpensive counter to Britain's vulnerable battleship-focused fleet. The response to the torpedo threat was to provide battleships with another assortment of light weapons that could quickly engage a large number of small, unarmored targets. The French firm Hotchkiss introduced a series of 37mm, 42mm, 47mm, and 57mm quick-firing guns in the 1880s to deal with the torpedo boat threat, but as torpedo boats grew in size a heavier 75mm gun was introduced in 1891. As designers added new weapons to counter each potential threat, battleships by the mid-1890s were being built with up to five classes of guns aboard, which added a great deal of unnecessary weight.

The problem of armor protection was initially solved simply with layers of wrought-iron plates over the warship's main battery and engine spaces, but the entire ship could not be armored because it would become dangerously top-heavy. Once genuine armor-piercing shells were introduced, French engineers led the way toward the greater use of steel in warship construction and the British development of compound steel armor in 1884 promised 50 percent better protection than iron plate. For a time, ship-builders simply increased the amount of compound armor carried. However, Britain and France took divergent approaches to perfecting armor layout. British designers favored a "central battery concept," where the center of the ship, including the main armament and machinery spaces, was protected by a very thick armor, but the bow and stern were virtually unarmored. The French took a different tack, preferring to distribute a wider armor belt at the waterline to protect against ramming and torpedo threats, since they felt close combat was a greater threat to the battleship than long-range gunnery. French designers preferred "tumblehome" hull forms, with hulls that bulged outward at the waterline, which offered greater protection against close-in attacks. The trade-off of the tumblehome hull though, was to reduce the amount of armor that could be carried on the upper decks in order to avoid instability.

By 1889, compound armor was rapidly becoming vulnerable to the new high-velocity armor-piercing shells and it appeared that the battleship might become a technological dinosaur. Yet another string of technological breakthroughs occurred in the 1890s that suddenly shifted the advantage back to the defense. In 1891, American engineers developed Harvey nickel-steel armor that was considerably more resiliant than compound armor, and the British began incorporating it in their new *Majestic*-class battleships. Five years later, German engineers developed Krupp steel plate and tests indicated that "Holtzer" armor-piercing shells could only penetrate Krupp armor at point-blank range.

Finally, the evolution of the battleship was also influenced by the efficiency and capability of naval propulsion plants. The steam engine had evolved from the single-stage engines of the 1860s to the compound engine of the 1870s, followed by the vertical triple expansion (VTE) engines of the 1880s, which reduced both the weight of the machinery and coal consumption. Boilers also evolved from the rectangular iron units of the 1860s to the steel cylindrical boilers of the 1870s, which raised ship speeds up to 15 knots. Naval engineers had been working to perfect high-pressure water tube boilers since the 1850s, but the first practical one was not installed in a warship until 1886. Several companies including Belleville, Thornycroft and Niclausse developed high-pressure water tube boilers in this period, with varying degrees of reliability and success – navies had to pick from this assortment based only upon limited testing. In 1889, the French Navy adopted the Belleville boiler and installed it on the battleship *Brennus*. The more conservative Royal Navy did not adopt Belleville boilers on battleships until 1896. On trials, these battleships of the mid-1890s with VTE engines and Belleville boilers were capable of 18 knots for four hours, with sustained speeds of 14–15 knots.

The *Poltava* fitting out in 1896, with 6-in guns not yet installed yet. Influenced by both American and French battleship design, the *Poltava*-class emphasized protection and was the first Russian battleship to mount Krupp armor. (Naval Historical Center, NH73114)

# RUSSIAN BATTLESHIPS

Russia had begun developing a major warship construction center at St Petersburg in 1704, and by the 1880s it was capable of building its own battleships. Indeed, St Petersburg had three naval yards for battleship construction: the New Admiralty yard, the Baltic Shipbuilding and Engineering Works, and the Franco-Russian Works at Galerniy Island. Although Russia's military-industrial base was still relatively small, it had the resources to produce most of the materials it needed for warship construction. Naval guns were built by the Obukhovskii Works (OSZ) and Putilov plants, armor was made by the Izhorskii Works and engine machinery by the Baltic Works. However, the fragile Russian industrial base could not handle surges in naval orders and often had to purchase quantities of armor plate, weapons and machinery from Britain, France, Germany and the United States. Warship designs were selected by the *Morskoi tekhnicheskii komitet* or MTK (Naval Technical Committee), but influential admirals in the Naval Ministry could and did tinker with the designs.

Russia began building its own ironclads in the 1860s and by 1876 it completed its first battleship, the *Petr Velikii*. It took the Russians over seven years to build the *Petr Velikii* and it was an expensive and frustrating experience. The Russian Navy did not order another battleship for another 13 years, until the accession of Tsar Aleksandr III in 1881 brought sweeping changes to the Naval Ministry. In April 1882, Aleksandr III approved the Twenty Year Program, which authorized the building of up to 24 battleships by 1902.

The MTK was tasked to design these new battleships in a period of rapid technological change and it often tried to hedge its bets by simultaneously pursuing different technical directions. In 1885, uncertain as to whether turrets or barbettes were better, the MTK took the simple expedient of building one of the new *Imperator Aleksandr II*-class battleships with 12-in/30-cal guns in turrets and the other with barbettes. In November 1890, the Naval Ministry ordered the MTK to develop two different design paths, one for a first-class battleship based on an improved *Imperator Aleksandr II*-class and another for a second-class battleship.

Launching of the battleship *Pobeda* ("Victory") at the Baltic Works in St Petersburg on May 10, 1900. This was the last of the *Peresvyet*-class battleships and it was commissioned on May 19, 1902 and promptly sent to Port Arthur. (Dmitri Malkov)

While the MTK was designing battleships, it was also making efforts to improve the firepower of its ships. In the early 1890s, Vice-Adm Stepan O. Makarov, chief inspector of naval artillery, proposed a major upgrade for Russian battleship armament. Makarov advocated developing a new 12-in gun that fired lighter shells with higher muzzle velocities in order to hit targets beyond traditional combat ranges. In conjunction with Canet, Obukhov designed the 12-in/40-cal M1895 to be the new primary weapon for Russian battleships.

The new gun extended the engagement range of Russian battleships from 5–6km to over 10km and increased muzzle velocity by 25–35 percent over previous models, as well as reducing reload time from 2–4 minutes to only 90 seconds. However, the bursting charges were substantially reduced in order to save weight on the shell, resulting in less "punch" when it hit its target. Makarov also advocated armor-piercing capped (APC) shells, which should have given Russian battleships a decisive edge, but due to cost few of

The French-built battleship *Tsesarevich* during her trials at Toulon in 1903. This battleship incorporated a "tumblehome" shaped hull, cellular armor and secondary guns in twin electric turrets. This was a very modern battleship for its day. (Naval Historical Center, NH63232)

these improved shells were purchased. Further, Makarov directed a junior officer, Semyon V. Panpushko, to perfect the explosive Melinite for use in shells. Panpushko discovered something that had eluded the Japanese – that acids within Melinite reacted with the steel in a shell casing and formed dangerous compounds – but he was blown to bits in November 1891. After Panpushko's death, the Russian Navy lost interest in Melinite and decided to retain gun cotton until a safer alternative could be found.

The design for the second-class battleship was completed in August 1891 and the New Admiralty yard began constructing a 10,000-ton battleship, the *Sissoi Veliki*, which incorporated all the latest innovations including four 12-in/40-cal guns in two barbettes, Harvey nickel-steel armor, Belleville boilers and high freeboard. Typical of the ever-changing Russian process of ship design, two years into construction the MTK ordered the *Sissoi Veliki* to be completed with turrets instead and changed both the types of 12-in and 6-in guns. Invariably, Russian battleships ended up overweight and over-budget. Once completed, the *Sissoi Veliki* was 1,500 tons heavier than expected, increasing the draught by 3½ feet – which caused her main armor belt to lie 4ins below the waterline. Thus the *Sissoi Veliki's* formidable 16-in-thick Harvey nickel-steel main armor belt was submerged underwater, leaving only the 5-in-thick upper belt for protection above the waterline. While the *Sissoi Veliki* was considered "second-rate," it did validate key design features and set the pattern for the Russian battle fleet that was evolving on the drawing boards in St Petersburg.

The battleship *Borodino* being launched on September 8, 1901 at the New Admiralty yard in St Petersburg. The *Borodino*-class was a Russian-built version of the *Tsesarevich* and the lead ship in the class cost 14.5 million rubles (about £1.8 million). (Dmitri Malkov)

Six months after work began on the *Sissoi Veliki*, the New Admiralty and Galerniy Island yards began work on the first-class battleships *Poltava*, *Petropavlovsk* and *Sevastopol*. The Naval Ministry requirement called for a 10,500-ton battleship with emphasis on armored protection, seaworthiness and a range of 11,000km. The MTK based some of the design on the American *Indiana*-class battleships with a flush-deck hull and high freeboard, but also partly on the French

battleship *Brennus*. The *Petropavlovsk*-class was also noteworthy for adopting French-style turrets for its 6-in secondary battery, but was somewhat regressive in using standard cylindrical boilers rather than the new Belleville boilers. The class was severely delayed by the inability of Russian industry to supply the 12-in/40-cal Pattern 1895 guns and armor plate on schedule, resulting in construction lasting seven years. Once completed, the *Petropavlovsk*-class battleships were fairly seaworthy and capable of 15–16 knots, although their new 12-in guns suffered from defects that impaired their firepower. The *Poltava* was the first Russian battleship to use Krupp armor from Germany, while the other two ships in the class used Harvey nickel-steel armor purchased from the United States. In most respects, the *Petropavlovsk*-class was a fairly successful design for its day and all three ships were duly sent to Port Arthur.

Despite their development of a fairly effective battleship design, the Naval Ministry decided to experiment with other variations of armament and armor on the next class of Russian battleships built for Far East service. Britain had commissioned two fast battleships of the *Centurion*-class in 1894, armed with 10-in guns. When the MTK began designing the next generation of Russian battleships in 1895, England was considered the likely enemy and the resulting *Peresvyet*-class was conceived as a fast "battleship-cruiser" that could act in anti-cruiser or commerce-raiding roles. The *Peresvyet*-class used the lighter 10-in/45-cal Pattern 1891 gun, which enabled the ships to carry 29 percent more main gun ammunition, but the rate of fire was disappointing. Work began on *Peresvyet* and *Oslyabya* in November 1895, and *Pobieda* in February 1899. In trials, all three ships demonstrated the ability to attain speeds of 18 knots with their Belleville boilers, which satisfied the requirement for a fast battleship. However, all three ships were grossly overweight, causing the armor belts to be submerged below the waterline when fully loaded. The *Peresvyet*-class were typical of the type of compromises that seem reasonable in a time of rapid technological transition but do not ultimately perform on the battlefield – the ships of this class were relatively fast and suited for anti-cruiser duties but lacked the firepower and protection to go toe-to-toe with a first-class battleship.

By early 1898, the Russian shipyards around St Petersburg had six battleships under construction but since average build time was over five years, the Naval Ministry turned to foreign yards to reach its goal of ten battleships for the Far East. The American shipbuilder Charles Henry Cramp, eager to gain a contract for both new battleships, traveled to St Petersburg and with the help of the US ambassador he peddled a design based on the American battleship *Iowa*. Cramp had already built four battleships for the US Navy and after some hesitation the MTK accepted a modified proposal. The contract signed in April 1898 required Cramp to build a 12,700-ton battleship in 30 months at a price of $4.36 million (£1.09 million). Construction began on the *Retvizan* in December 1898 at the Cramp yard in Philadelphia.

The *Retvizan* was built with a flush-deck hull and used French-designed 12-in gun turrets, but kept the secondary armament in armored casemates. Both the turrets and the main armament were built in Russia and shipped to Philadelphia for installation. Cramp favored the new French-designed Niclausse high-pressure water tube boilers – which he claimed offered improved performance and reliability over the Belleville boiler – so the MTK reluctantly agreed to try this novel steam plant on the *Retvizan*. Bethlehem Iron

# BORODINO

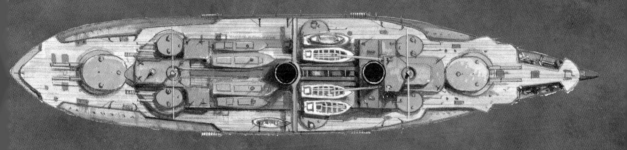

## SPECIFICATIONS

Laid down: May 23, 1900, New
  Admiralty yard, St Petersburg
Launched: September 8, 1901
Commissioned: August 23, 1904
Standard displacement: 14,181 tons
Length: 397' overall (121m)
Width: 76' 1" (23.2m)
Draught: 27'–29' 2" maximum
  (8.24–8.9m)
Machinery: 20 x Belleville boilers, 2 x
  4-cylinder VTE engines; 16,300ihp
Speed: 17.5 knots maximum
Coal: 787 tons standard load/ 1,235
  tons full load
Range: 2,370 miles at 10 knots with
  standard load

Armor:
Type of armor: Krupp
Armor protection:
Main belt: 6–7.64in (152–194mm)
Upper belt: 6in (152mm)
Bow & stern: 4–5.7in (102–145mm)
12-inch turrets: 10in (254mm) sides,
  2.5in (63mm) roof
6-in gun turrets: 6in (152mm) sides
Conning tower: 8in (203mm) sides,
  1.5in (37mm) roof
Main deck: 1in (25mm)

Armament:
4 x 305/40mm guns (total 240
  rounds) Rate of fire: 1 round/90 sec
12 x 152/45mm guns (total 2,160
  rounds)
20 x 75/50mm guns (26,000 rounds)
20 x 47/43mm guns
2 x 37/23mm guns
4 x 7.62mm machine guns
4 x 381mm torpedo tubes

Crew: 866
Cost: 14.57 million rubles
  (£1.8 million)

The battleship *Retvizan* at the Brooklyn Navy yard in 1901 (note US submarine *Holland* in the foreground). The *Retvizan* used a flush-deck hull unlike the French-influenced battleships in the Russian Navy and proved to be a very tough ship in battle. (Naval Historical Center, NH53457)

Works supplied Krupp-style armor plate. Despite Cramp's claims, he failed to complete the *Retvizan* on time and its Niclausse boilers proved unable to deliver the 18-knot speed promised. Furthermore, the Niclausse boilers proved to be dangerous and unreliable. On the plus side, the *Retvizan* was only slightly overweight so its main belt armor was not compromised and its armament proved satisfactory in gunnery trials.

Another foreigner eager to hawk his designs to the Russian Naval Ministry was Antoine-Jean Amable Lagane, director of the French shipyard Forges et Chantiers de la Méditerranée in La Seyne (Toulon). He presented the MTK with a design for a battleship based on the French *Jauréguiberry*. Lagane was aided by the support of the Francophile Grand Duke Aleksei Aleksandrovich, brother of Tsar Aleksandr III and nominally head of the Imperial Navy. In July 1898 the Naval Ministry signed a contract with Lagane to build a 12,900-ton battleship in 42 months at a cost of 30.28 million francs (£1.47 million). Construction began on the *Tsesarevich* in May 1899 but like Cramp, Lagane failed to meet the schedule and the ship required 51 months to complete. The *Tsesarevich* had a high-forecastle hull with a curved tumblehome shape – the beam of the ship narrowed from the waterline to the upper deck, in order to reduce the weight of the upper deck – which French designers believed would allow greater freeboard and improved seaworthiness. The *Tsesarevich* also incorporated a 9.8-in-thick main belt of Krupp armor using Louis-Émile Bertin's "cellular" approach to protection, which enhanced the ship's ability to survive damage and remain afloat. The Belleville boilers that the MTK had insisted on proved far more reliable than Cramp's Niclausse boilers and in trials the *Tsesarevich* achieved speeds of over 18 knots. In virtually every respect, the *Tsesarevich* was the best Russian battleship built prior to the Russo-Japanese War.

The Russian Naval Technical Committee (MTK) and Grand Duke Aleksandrovich were very impressed with the design and wanted to build a similar type of battleship in the yards of St Petersburg. Even before the contract with Lagane was signed, the MTK directed Dmitri V. Skvortsov, a designer for the New Admiralty yard, to take the sketches from Lagane's technical proposals and turn them into a Russian version. Skvortsov had to increase the designed displacement by 600 tons over the *Tsesarevich* since Russian-built turrets and engine-room equipment were heavier than the French-built versions, but in three weeks he produced plans for the new *Borodino*-class battleships. After eight months of dithering, on March 23, 1899 the MTK finally chose a modified Skvortsov design and placed an order for three new battleships: the *Borodino* from the New

Admiralty yard, the *Imperator Aleksandr III* from the Baltic Works and the *Orel* from the Galerniy yard. Construction work began on the first two in July 1899 and the third in March 1900. Two more ships of the class, *Kniaz Suvarov* and *Slava*, were ordered in 1900. Although the *Borodino*-class was outwardly similar to the *Tsesarevich*, the increase in their displacement had a major impact on their combat-effectiveness.

# JAPANESE BATTLESHIPS

The IJN ordered its first armored warship from Britain in 1875. Despite the satisfaction with the quality of British-built ships and weapons, Japan's Naval Ministry turned to France for assistance in building up its fleet. In 1885 the Ministry obtained the services of the French naval designer Louis-Émile Bertin, who helped the Japanese to jump-start their naval construction program at the Yokosuka Naval Yard near Tokyo and to organize the main fleet base at Sasebo. In addition to drawing upon the high level of French technical expertise in explosives, engine machinery and armor plate, Japan's Naval Ministry was attracted to the *Jeune École* doctrine that appeared to offer a shortcut for resource-poor navies to match stronger opponents with explosive shells and torpedoes.

Yet even with Bertin's assistance, Japan could not begin constructing battleships in its own yards until May 1905, too late for the confrontation with Russia. However, the Naval Ministry funded several technical initiatives that could provide significant tactical advantages to its British-built battleships. In 1888, a Japanese naval officer in France covertly acquired samples of the explosive Melinite, which were brought back to Japan and reconstituted at the Kure naval arsenal as *Shimosa* in 1892. Like the British explosive Lyddite, *Shimosa* created strong over-pressures and heat when it detonated, which could be very destructive to unarmored structures. Apparently, the Ministry realized that its Holtzer-type armor-piercing (AP) rounds purchased from France were unlikely to penetrate the latest Krupp armor on Russian battleships, so it decided to develop a new type of anti-armor round relying on blast more than penetration. A new thin-jacketed steel shell was developed, dubbed *furoshiki*, and packed with 19.3kg of *Shimosa* – four times the size of the standard bursting charge on an AP shell. The Ministry also developed the *Ijuin* fuse for the new shell, which caused detonation on impact. British tests with Lyddite shells against the old ironclad *Belleisle* in 1900 indicated that high explosives could tear great holes in the hull and destroy all the fire mains and hand pumps, making it difficult for the crew to extinguish fires on deck. During

The battleship *Yashima*, built at Newcastle in 1894–1897. Like her sister ship *Fuji*, the *Yashima* was an improved version of the British *Royal Sovereign*-class. (Naval Historical Center, NH58968)

# MIKASA

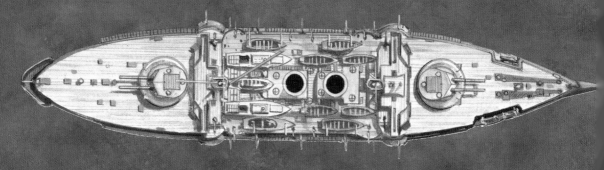

## SPECIFICATIONS

Laid down: January 24, 1899,
 Armstrong-Whitworth, Elswick, UK
Launched: November 8, 1900
Commissioned: March 1, 1902
Standard displacement: 15,140 tons
Length: 432' overall (131.7m)
Width: 76' (23.2m)
Draught: 27' (8.28m)
Machinery: 25 x Belleville boilers, 2 x
 3-cylinder VTE engines; 15,000ihp
Speed: 18 knots maximum
Coal: 700 tons standard load/1,521
 tons full load
Range: 7,000 miles at 10 knots with
 standard load

Armor:
Type of armor: Krupp
Armor protection:
Main belt: 4–9in (101–228mm)
Upper belt: 6in (152mm)
Bow & stern: 4in (102mm)
12-in turrets: 10in (254mm)
 sides, 2.5in (63mm) roof
Barbettes: 14–16in (352–403mm)
Casemates: 2–6in (50–152mm)
Conning tower: 14in (352mm) sides,
 1.5in (37mm) roof
Main deck: 1in (25mm)

Armament:
4 x 305/40mm guns (total 240
 rounds) Rate of fire: 1 round/min
14 x 152/40mm guns (total 2,800
 rounds)
20 x 75mm guns (3,000 rounds)
4 x 47/43mm guns (6,000 rounds)
4 x 450mm torpedo tubes

Crew: 830
Cost: ¥8.8 million (£880,000)

the test, the battleship HMS *Majestic* achieved 40 percent hits against the stationary target at a range of 1.5km – reaffirming the notion that a battleship action could only be decisive at short ranges.

The Japanese Naval Ministry ordered two *Fuji*-class battleships from England in 1893, with *Fuji* built during 1894–97 at Thames Ironworks & Shipbuilding Company and *Yashima* built at Armstrong-Whitworth's yard. The *Fuji*-class battleships were based upon the *Royal Sovereign*-class battleships, but substituted lighter 12-in guns in turrets instead of the 13.5-in guns in barbettes on the British battleships. The saving in weight on armament enabled the builders to add more cylindrical boilers than the British used, increasing engine horsepower from 9,000 on the British ships to 14,000 on the *Fuji* and *Yashima*, giving them a 2-knot speed advantage. The Japanese also

substituted Harvey nickel-steel armor during construction of both battleships. Japan's British-built battleships had a distinct advantage in hull form and stability, thanks to the British introduction of model testing in 1870.

When the Sino-Japanese War began in August 1894 the IJN had to rely upon its cruiser force to defeat China's battleships. At the Battle of the Yalu River, the outgunned Japanese cruisers used a deluge of medium-caliber fire to incapacitate the two Chinese battleships; the *Ting Yuan* was hit over 200 times and *Chen Yuan* over 100 times, but the armor was not penetrated on either ship. Instead, the Japanese shells set numerous fires on the Chinese battleships and forced them to withdraw after four hours of close combat, at ranges of 2.7km–5.5km. Eventually, the Japanese fleet was able to corner the damaged Chinese battleships at Wei-hai-wei and sink one with a torpedo and the other surrendered. The lesson that Japan's naval leaders learned from these two naval actions was that their fleet needed heavy guns with higher rates of fire and better penetration, mounted on hulls that had sufficient armored protection to minimize damage at ranges of 5.5km.

Once Yamamoto's "Six-Six" program was approved in 1896, the next four Japanese battleships were based upon the *Majestic*-class, which were easily the best all-round battleships of the 1890s. Both the two *Shikishima*-class battleships, the *Asahi* and the *Mikasa*, were fairly similar to the *Majestic*-class but the Japanese opted for subtle qualitative improvements that would give them an edge in performance. The major difference was that the Japanese chose Belleville boilers instead of the standard cylindrical boilers, which gave increased horsepower yielding up to 2 knots of greater speed. All the Japanese battleships were built with Harvey nickel-steel armor, except for the *Mikasa*, which was the only one to receive Krupp armor. The "Six-Six" program was completed when *Mikasa* was commissioned in March 1902 and it was made the flagship of the Combined Fleet at Sasebo.

In order to defeat the Chinese battleships in 1894, the Japanese cruisers closed to less than 5,000 meters and peppered them with 4.7-in and 6-in rounds. Here, the *Chen Yuen* displays multiple shell impacts (white circles) on her upperworks, funnels and gun turrets – none of which actually penetrated her compound armor. Instead, the barrage shattered the morale of the poorly trained Chinese crew, who opted to surrender. This Japanese tactic would be repeated at Tsushima. (Naval Historical Center, NH88892)

# STRATEGIC SITUATION

*At last! An ice-free port!*

Tsar Nicholas writing in his diary about Port Arthur,
March 27, 1898

OPPOSITE
Admiral Togo Heihachiro
(1847–1934), Commander
of the Combined Fleet since
December 1903. Togo had
seen considerable combat
in the Satsuma Navy before
joining the new Imperial
Japanese Navy in 1871. He
was sent to train in England
and proved an adept student.
During the Sino-Japanese
War, Togo commanded the
cruiser *Naniwa* and fought
at the Battle of the Yalu
River. After the war he was
promoted to Vice-Admiral in
1898 and then Admiral in
1904. Togo was a tough and
ruthless commander, who
could be merciless to his
opponents. (Museum of
Fine Arts, Boston)

In 1903, the Russian Empire had an annual revenue of £214 million, of which £12.3 million was spent on the fleet. With a new battleship costing over £1 million in the late 1890s, Russia could afford to build or purchase up to three battleships per year. However, Russia had to maintain three separate fleets in the Baltic Sea, Black Sea and Pacific, which made it very difficult to mass its available naval resources against a single opponent. Unlike Japan, Russia had several potential enemies, including Germany and the Ottoman Empire, for which it had to retain forces in place to act as a deterrent. Under the "For the Needs of the Far East" Program adopted on January 8, 1898, the Naval Ministry changed its policy and decided to deploy greater assets to the Far East, including ten battleships, in order to support the Tsar's expansionist policies. The Baltic and Black Sea fleets were reduced to defensive roles, with priority given to new construction for the Pacific Squadron. At the start of the Russo-Japanese War, Russia had 17 operational battleships: seven were stationed in the Pacific, one was en route to the Pacific, one was in the Mediterranean Sea, three were in the Baltic and five were in the Black Sea. In addition, five *Borodino*-class battleships were under construction in St Petersburg and were approaching completion.

The squadron at Port Arthur, under the command of Vice-Adm Oskar V. Stark, was the main component of Russian naval power in the Far East, although a powerful

# TECHNICAL SPECIFICATIONS

Although the Russian and Japanese battleships used in combat in 1904–05 were a heterogeneous collection of vessels rather than a single distinct class, they were built with roughly equivalent capabilities in terms of firepower, armor protection, maneuverability and communications.

## FIREPOWER

The battleship was inherently built around its ability to act as a stable gun platform. However, in order to use its firepower against an enemy ship, a battleship first had to spot the target. In the Yellow Sea area, lookouts in the combat top of a battleship could detect a battleship-size target out to about 27km in daylight with clear visibility, although haze or morning fog could reduce this to less than 9km. Most navies in this period avoided gunnery duels at night, and instead preferred to use these conditions for torpedo boat attacks.

Once a target was detected, the range to the target had to be determined and the data given to the battleship's gun crews. Most Russian battleships relied upon the Liuzhol rangefinder, introduced in the 1880s and effective out to 3.6km. In the mid-1890s the Royal Navy began to revolutionize naval gunnery with the introduction of telescopes, improved mechanical rangefinders and a technique of continuous aim that compensated for the roll of the ship. In 1899, the Royal Navy conducted its first long-range gunnery exercise out to 5.5km using the new sights and they improved their hit rate at 1.4km to

A 6-in gun destined for *Mikasa*. The Elswick 6-in/40-cal gun was typical of the medium-caliber weapons that began appearing on battleships in the late 1880s, which were intended to make up in volume of fire what they lacked in range and throw weight. (Vickers Photographic Archive)

A Japanese 6-in/40-cal gun mount and crew. The British-built battleships mounted most of their secondary armament in armored casemates, rather than in turrets as used by French battleships. (Museum of Fine Arts, Boston)

80 percent. The British firm Barr & Stroud introduced the FA2 rangefinder in 1901 and the superior FA3 in 1903, for which the Japanese became the first foreign customers. The Japanese were quick to adopt these new British-made devices and techniques, which drastically improved the effectiveness of their naval gunnery. All the Japanese battleships were fitted with four Barr & Stroud FA3 coincidence rangefinders, which offered improved accuracy out to 7.3km but which had a significant margin of error beyond that range. The Japanese battleships were also retrofitted with telescopic sights with 24-power magnification by 1903. The Russian Navy had less access to British technology and gunnery tactics and it was thus slower to adopt the new advances. By the start of the war in 1904, *Retvizan* and the *Tsesarevich* each had one Barr & Stroud FA2 rangefinder and the *Borodino*-class later received one Barr & Stroud FA3 rangefinder, but none of the Russian battleships in the 1st Pacific Squadron had telescopic sights. The battleships in the 2nd Pacific Squadron were equipped with the Perepelkin optical sight just before sailing and their crews were not trained in its use.

Aside from the *Peresvyet*-class, all the first-line battleships that fought in the Russo-Japanese War used 12-in/40-cal guns as their primary weapon. On the *Borodino*-class battleships, the main armament consisted of four 12-in/40-cal guns mounted in twin turrets fore and aft. The Canét-Obukhoff Model 1892 12-in/40-cal gun could fire a 331kg high explosive (HE) shell or armor-piercing (AP) round out to a maximum range of 14,640m at 15° elevation. However, a Russian battleship firing a four-gun broadside under ideal conditions[5] only had a 10 percent chance of scoring one hit on another battleship at a range of 9km, against a probability of 40 percent at 3.6km or less. While Russian APC shells could theoretically penetrate the main belt armor on a *Mikasa*-class battleship out to maximum range, very few of these shells were available in 1904 and both sides had to make do with steel AP shells and HE shells. The Russian 12-in AP shells were lighter than Japanese 12-in AP shells (331kg vs 386kg) but consequently had better muzzle velocity (792m/sec vs 732m/sec). Neither side's 12-in guns could reliably penetrate the main armor belt of their opponents at battle ranges beyond 5km.

"JAPANESE NAVY."
Lieutenant and Men with 6 inch Quick Firing Gun.

5   Gunnery conducted under daylight conditions with good visibility. The target is a battleship target that is moving at less than 15 knots broadside to the firing ship.

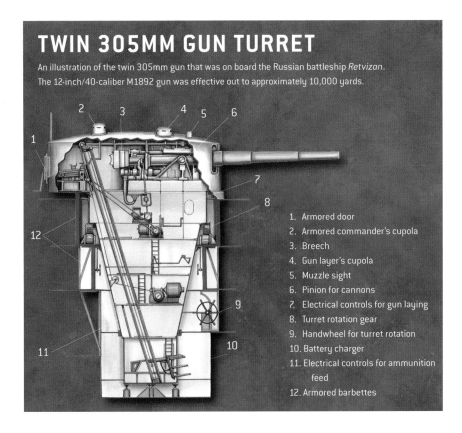

# TWIN 305MM GUN TURRET

An illustration of the twin 305mm gun that was on board the Russian battleship *Retvizan*.
The 12-inch/40-caliber M1892 gun was effective out to approximately 10,000 yards.

1. Armored door
2. Armored commander's cupola
3. Breech
4. Gun layer's cupola
5. Muzzle sight
6. Pinion for cannons
7. Electrical controls for gun laying
8. Turret rotation gear
9. Handwheel for turret rotation
10. Battery charger
11. Electrical controls for ammunition feed
12. Armored barbettes

Russian 12-in/40-cal guns were installed in French-style electrically powered turrets. The rate of fire on Russian guns was lower than that of Japanese battleships, usually only one aimed round every 90–120 seconds. Rounds were brought up from shell rooms on electrical hoists and the magazine held anywhere from 232 to 308 rounds. The projectile was then loaded into the gun with bagged propellant charges totaling 100kg of black powder. Russian ammunition handling was fairly safe – accidental explosions were uncommon – due to their use of wet gun cotton as an explosive and black powder as a propellant. Russian 12-in guns were still fired using lanyards, which were slower than the new electrical firing switches on Japanese battleships, but less vulnerable to battle damage.

All six Japanese battleships were armed with four British-built 12-in/40-cal guns that had a rate of fire of 1rpm. The Elswick-Armstrong Pattern G 12-in/40-cal gun could fire a 386kg HE or AP shell out to a maximum of 13.7km at an elevation of 15°. Despite slighter shorter range than their opponents, the Japanese 12-in shells carried much larger burster charges (both *Shimosa* and black powder) than their Russian counterparts, which caused greater blast damage. However, *Shimosa* was considered something of a "secret weapon" and the Japanese had not trained with it much before the war to avoid alerting the Russians to its introduction into service. The Japanese 12-in AP round carried a 19kg burster charge versus 5.3kg on the Russian AP round and the Japanese HE round carried a 39kg charge versus only 12.4kg for the Russian HE round. The Japanese also used cordite as a propellant, but this proved very accident-prone in combat.

The secondary armament on Russian battleships consisted of 11 or 12 6-in/45-cal Canét M1891 guns, mounted either in armored casemates or electrically powered twin turrets. Mounting secondary guns in turrets was a French idea that was ahead of its time, but the early 6-in turrets on the *Petropavlovsk*-class had numerous engineering defects. These French-designed 6-in guns were excellent weapons with a maximum range of 11.5km, although their effective range was around 5km. With a typical arc of fire of only 120–150°, no more than six guns could fire at a single target and each gun had a sustained rate of fire of 2–4rpm. Unlike Japanese 6-in guns, which were only issued with HE rounds, the Russian 6-in guns were also provided with AP rounds that could penetrate some of the thinner armor plating on the bow and stern of Japanese battleships at ranges of 2–3km. Japanese battleships carried 10–14 6-in/40-cal Elswick-designed quick-firing guns, which could fire a 45kg HE shell out to a maximum of 9,140m. Although the Elswick guns had less range than the Canét guns, they had nearly double the rate of fire, some 5–6rpm. Secondary armament was often fired under local control and tended to be less accurate than the main batteries, but made it up for it in volume of rounds fired. While the 6-in rounds could not sink a battleship, the HE rounds posed a significant threat to exposed crew members on a ship's bridge and upper decks.

A large portion of a battleship's armament was designed to deter or defeat torpedo boat attacks. Except for the older *Petropavlovsk*-class, the Russian battleships carried a light battery consisting of 16–20 75mm guns, 10–20 47mm guns and 8–28 37mm guns scattered in the fighting tops, the superstructure and hull embrasures. The elderly Hotchkiss-designed 37mm and 47mm guns had high rates of fire with 15–32rpm, but they could only engage targets at a maximum of 2–4km and their small shells lacked the stopping power to defeat larger torpedo boats. In order to meet this threat, the Russians adopted the Canét-designed 75mm/50-cal M1891 and the Japanese adopted the Elswick-built 12-pounder QF Pattern N (75mm) gun to engage torpedo boats out to 5km. However, at night, 90cm searchlights could only detect torpedo boats out to 3.6km. Japanese ships carried a somewhat smaller light battery, usually with 16–20 75mm, 4–12 50mm or 4–6 40mm guns. The main torpedo threats in the Far East theater – the Japanese 356mm Type 26 and 450mm Type 37 and the Russian 381mm Model 1898 – had maximum ranges varying between only 650 and 1,000m, which made it very difficult for them to get within attack range of an alert and well-defended battleship.

The forward 12-in gun turret on *Mikasa*, with starboard searchlight platform visible. Each 12-in gun turret had 120 rounds in its magazine, which was only enough for one hour of sustained combat. Long-range gunnery duels, such as Yellow Sea, tended to use up the limited main gun ammunition supply without achieving much. (Author's photo)

## PROTECTION

In several respects, Russian battleships enjoyed advantages in armored protection over their opponents. Whereas eight of the 12 Russian battleships sent to the Pacific used Krupp armor, the *Mikasa* was the only one of the six Japanese battleships to mount this latest type of armored protection. The *Tsesarevich*- and *Borodino*-class battleships also incorporated a sophisticated "cellular" layout of their armor that increased the ship's ability to absorb damage. As it turned out, both Harvey and Krupp armor plate proved to be very difficult to penetrate at ranges beyond 5km, but the battleship had two critical weaknesses that were difficult to protect against: danger from fire, and the splinter or fragmentation threat to exposed bridge personnel.

Russian battleships emphasized protecting the ship's waterline. The main armored belt on the *Tsesarevich* was 9.84ins thick amidships and tapered to 6.3ins at the ends, supplemented by a 7.9-in-thick upper belt. The armored belts on the *Borodino*-class were reduced to only 7.64ins thick in the main and 6ins thick in the upper belt. However, the tendency of Russian designs to be heavier than expected seriously compromised the armor belts on both the *Borodino*-class and the *Peresvyet*-class, both of which were so overweight that all or most of their main belt was submerged below the waterline at normal displacement. In contrast, Japan's British-built battleships employed the central battery concept in armor, emphasizing protection of a larger portion of the center of the ship.

Looking aft on the *Mikasa*, toward the rear searchlight platform. Most of the casualties would occur in this area near the spar deck and the gun casemates below were open in the back, exposing gunners to possible splinter injuries. (Author's photo)

The main armor belt on the *Asahi* was 8.2ft tall, compared to only 6.5ft tall on the *Tsesarevich*. In addition to armor plate, additional protection was afforded by arranging coal bunkers around critical areas such as the engine rooms and some magazines.

Despite thick armored belts, early battleships were highly vulnerable to fire damage due to cluttered superstructures and spar decks, crammed with inflammable ventilator shafts and wooden boats. Although the boats were usually filled with water prior to going into combat and excess woodwork removed, a great deal of wood and canvas remained stored in the upper superstructure which could be ignited by high explosive rounds. The bridge personnel on battleships were also terribly exposed to shell fragments and only a handful could fit inside the armored conning towers. A single shell could wipe out the fleet commander and his staff, as well as key members of the battleship's crew. Japanese battleships did have thicker protection on their conning towers – 14ins versus 6–10ins. However, Vice-Adm Togo chose to command from outside the conning tower on the *Mikasa*, providing better situational awareness but eschewing survivability. Other Japanese commanders remained inside their conning towers. Russian conning towers proved to be too small, and with wide apertures vulnerable to splinters.

# MANEUVERABILITY

The Vertical Triple Expansion (VTE) engines that powered the battleships on each side were not capable of particularly high speeds, but they were fairly reliable and economical on coal use. A battleship such as *Tsesarevich*, with a normal load of 800 tons of coal, used only 3 tons of coal per hour at a speed of 12 knots, giving it a potential range of 5,000km with one load of fuel. However, a battleship moving at 18 knots

| User | Type | Maximum Range (m) | Rate of Fire (rounds/min) | Projectiles | Penetration of Krupp-type armor |
|---|---|---|---|---|---|
| | 12-in/40-cal M1895 (Canét/Obukhov) | 14,640 @ 15° elevation | 0.7 | HE, AP: 331kg | 3,660m – 251mm<br>5,490m – 201mm<br>7,320m – 159mm<br>9,140m – 129mm |
| | 12-in/40-cal Pattern G (Elswick-Armstrong) | 13,700 @ 15° elevation | 1 | HE, AP, Common: 386kg | |
| | 10-in/45-cal M1891 (Obukhov) | 20,486 @ 30° elevation | 0.7 | HE, AP: 225kg | 3,660m – 220mm<br>5,490m – 176mm<br>7,320m – 141mm<br>9,140m – 109mm |

The *Mikasa*'s vertical triple expansion (VTE) engine. Developed in the early 1880s, the VTE provided a fairly economical propulsion plant for pre-dreadnought battleships but limited their typical combat speeds to about 15 knots. (Vickers Photographic Archive)

would consume 15 tons of coal per hour. Damage to the ship's funnels could also greatly increase coal expenditure; when *Tsesarevich* had its funnels riddled by shell fragments at the Battle of the Yellow Sea, this increased its coal consumption to 20 tons per hour, which forced it to seek shelter in a neutral port before it ran out of fuel.

The Russian Navy was quick to realize the potential advantage of high-pressure Belleville boilers and adopted them on the *Peresvyet*-class battleships, ahead of both the Japanese and British navies. The engineering plant on the *Borodino*-class battleships consisted of two VTE engines with 20 Belleville boilers, capable of producing 15,800–16,300ihp. On trials in the Baltic, the *Borodino*-class ships achieved maximum speeds of 18 knots for short durations, but their maximum sustained speed was more like 15 knots in service. The *Mikasa*, with two VTE engines and 25 Belleville boilers, was rated at 16,340ihp in trials and capable of 18 knots, but in reality her normal maximum speed in combat was also 15 knots. Even with antifouling paint on the hull, after only six months of operations in tropical waters the drag from marine growths could reduce speed by 2 knots, so lengthy blockade operations off Port Arthur served to wear down the battleships' optimum performance. The speed of Russian battleships also suffered from operational circumstances: the battleships in the 1st Pacific Squadron had numerous mechanical deficiencies due to the limited maintenance facilities at Port Arthur, while the battleships in the 2nd Pacific Squadron had their speed badly reduced by hull fouling and excess weight. Those ships built with tumblehome hulls were also plagued by stability problems, particularly in high-speed turning. During the *Aleksandr III*'s trials in the Baltic in October 1903, a moderate turn to port at high speed resulted in a sudden 15° heeling and the ship began taking in water through its hull gun embrasures.

Russian battleships, expected to operate far from home, generally carried 15–40 percent more coal than their IJN counterparts, giving them better operational range. The operational mobility of IJN battleships was also inhibited by a severe shortage of high-grade coal. Japanese domestic coal was poor quality and the IJN relied on imported coal from Britain. At the start of the war, the IJN had only 650,000 tons of coal stockpiled, yet Togo's six battleships and 16 cruisers consumed over 10,000 tons of coal per week even at modest speeds. Britain did provide an additional 500,000 tons of Welsh coal just before the attack on Port Arthur, somewhat easing the

The battleship *Mikasa*, which mounted four 12-in/40-cal main guns, 14 6-in/40-cal secondary guns, and 20 75mm and eight 47mm guns for close-in defense. Despite this large amount of weaponry, *Mikasa* could only bring a small portion of its armament into play in any engagement beyond 6,000 meters. (Naval Historical Center, NH58973)

Combined Fleet's fuel concerns. Nevertheless, as the war dragged on into its second year, Togo had to watch his fuel consumption in order to have enough left for the main action expected when the Baltic Fleet arrived.

Overall, neither side had any real advantage in maneuverability over its opponents, although the Japanese battleships benefited from better maintenance facilities available at Sasebo. In tactical terms, the battleships were generally restricted to operating at 14 knots in formation, with short bursts of 15 knots that greatly increased their coal consumption.

# COMMUNICATIONS

Until 1899, battleships had relied upon signal flags for inter-ship communications and with good visibility conditions, signal flags could be read out to 7km. At night, flashing lights could also be used to send messages, but these were slow. Wireless radio communications became feasible in 1895 and four years later the Russian battleship *Tri Sviatitelia* of the Black Sea Fleet became the first warship in the world equipped with radio, although the Popov set initially only had a range of 5–10km. By 1902, all three *Poltava*-class battleships in the Far East were outfitted with Popov sets and the *Borodino*-class carried German-built Slaby-Arco radio sets. Early radio sets were extremely heavy – up to 6 tons – and even by 1905 were only capable of intermittent contact out to a maximum of 60km. Fleet communications over wireless were sent by Morse code in either enciphered or plain text and were fairly slow. The IJN began equipping their battleships with Marconi wireless sets after 1901, but the early ship-mounted sets were very unreliable, and limited to transmission ranges of 15–80km. Nevertheless, Togo was heavily dependent upon wireless communications both to conduct a distant blockade of Port Arthur and to watch for the arrival of the Baltic Fleet. Without radio, Togo would have had to expend his limited coal supply in months of patrolling, leaving little for the main event. The Russian Navy had the ability to jam Japanese wireless communications at least temporarily, but failed to do so.

# THE COMBATANTS

*To lead untrained people to war is to throw them away.*

Confucius (551–479 BC)

## THE RUSSIAN BATTLESHIP CREW

Russian sailors in 1893. The
Russian Navy was hindered
by a rigidly enforced caste
system that soured relations
between officers and enlisted
personnel. (Naval Historical
Center, NH72166)

Most Russian battleships had crews of 715–775 men, but the larger *Borodino*-class had a complement of 825. Russian battleships had only half as many officers as their Japanese counterparts, typically 23–28 officers. Each battleship also had about 60 petty officers. Like Japanese battleships, most of the crew was divided into gunnery and engineering divisions, but unlike the Japanese the Russians made little effort to build team spirit. Russian battleship crews were split into a rigid hierarchy between ranks that reflected the class-consciousness of Tsarist Russia.

Russian enlisted sailors were all conscripts, inducted at age 21 for seven years of active service and three years as reservists. Each year, roughly 9,000 sailors were inducted; many were from rural provinces and had never even seen the ocean before. About one-third of the conscripts were illiterate, which made training in technical subjects difficult. Sailors drafted from cities such as St Petersburg or Moscow

Russian sailors in 1893. The Russian Navy was hindered by a rigidly enforced caste system that soured relations between officers and enlisted personnel. (Naval Historical Center, NH72166)

were better educated but also more likely to be exposed to radical anti-regime ideas. Crews stationed in the Baltic spent much of the year in barracks ashore, with little time spent at sea. Once aboard ship, officers and NCOs often treated sailors poorly, with verbal abuse and corporal punishment the norm on many ships. Enlisted pay and chances for promotion were negligible. Naval rations for the enlisted were inadequate, and poor-quality food was the immediate cause of the mutiny on the battleship *Potemkin* in the Black Sea in May 1905.

Most Russian naval cadets entered the Naval Academy in St Petersburg at age 16–18 and by the 1890s the training period was reduced to three years. Class sizes were small: usually 50 cadets were accepted each year and entry was only open to the nobility or to sons of officers or government officials. Unlike the homogenous Japanese officer corps, the Russian Navy exemplified the ethnic and religious diversity of the Tsarist Empire: a significant percentage of officers were Lutherans of Baltic German extraction, and there were a number of Catholic Polish officers too. Although many Russian officers came from St Petersburg or the Baltic region, significant numbers also came from central and southern Russia. Once commissioned, Russian naval officers trained under a system known as *tsenz*, introduced in the 1880s to ensure that officers were qualified in a variety of duties. In actuality, the *tsenz* system encouraged a "ticket-punching" mentality among Russian officers, with emphasis upon meeting the minimum requirements for promotion. Unlike Japanese officers, who were intended to be generalists, Russian officers were usually specialists in gunnery or navigation, encouraged by membership in elite groups such as the Corps of Navigators (KFSH) and the officers from the top half of their academy class went to battleship and cruiser duty, while mediocrities were often assigned to staff and training slots. A junior officer on a battleship was usually a specialist in artillery, torpedoes or navigation. Most Russian battleship captains in the Far East were about two years older than their Japanese counterparts; Shchensnovich on the *Retvizan*

Russian sailors being issued their grog ration on the cruiser *Dmitri Donskoi* (scuttled after Tsushima). Increasing the daily ration of vodka was the only material incentive that the Imperial Russian Navy had to offer its sailors for better performance of their duties. (Naval Historical Center, NH72171)

was 52 and Grigorovich on the *Tsesarevich* was 51. On the other hand, most of the captains of the battleships at Port Arthur had been in command for at least two years.

Aboard ship, Russian officers kept their distance from enlisted sailors and one sailor on *Oslyabya* said his officers "didn't even know our names." Officers ate their own, better rations in their wardroom, drinking wine or champagne, caring little about whether the crew had enough food or if the filthy stokers could get regular showers to clean off. On some ships, martinet-style officers allowed their sailors to remain dirty as long as the decks were constantly scrubbed clean. This type of dysfunctional relationship – although not universal – was common enough to destroy any respect Russian sailors had for their officers, and it would contribute first to defeat, then revolution.

Unlike the IJN, which built morale on love of country and devotion to the Emperor, the Russian Navy tried to bolster shipboard morale with religion. Each battleship had an Orthodox priest assigned and every duty day started with mandatory group prayer on deck. Before going into battle, the priest also attempted to strengthen sailors' resolve with further prayers, but this tended to increase the innate Russian tendency toward fatalism. Furthermore, the Catholics and Lutherans among the crews resented being force-fed Orthodox theology.

The crews stationed at Port Arthur at the beginning of the war were much better trained and disciplined than the reinforcements that were later sent from the Baltic in Vice-Adm Rozhestvensky's 2nd Pacific Squadron. Many of the crews had considerable Far East experience under their belts – including the Boxer Rebellion – and were experienced "China hands." However, service in the Far East also had its share of distractions for Western sailors, which undermined readiness. On the night of the Japanese attack on Port Arthur, many of the crews were ashore, prowling the bars on Pushkin Street or in brothels such as the "American Legation." Meanwhile, the squadron commander, Vice-Adm Oskar V. Stark, was hosting a party aboard the flagship *Petropavlovsk*.

At least the Pacific Squadron was well trained in gunnery. The squadron's gunnery officer, Lt Andrey C. Myakishev, had made great efforts to develop salvo-firing procedures through a series of long-range gunnery exercises out to 7.3km, which was more realistic than the sub-caliber training used by the Japanese. When war came, the crews in the Far East knew how to shoot and to steam in formation. In contrast, the crews that formed the 2nd Pacific Squadron were primarily composed of the 1904 class of conscripts, as well as reservists recalled to the colors and various misfits and troublemakers from other units in the Baltic Fleet. However, one exception was the crew of the *Aleksandr III*, which comprised a large draft from the Marine Equipage Battalion, an elite naval unit in the Imperial Guard.[6] Rozhestvensky's crews were sent off to the Far East post-haste, with little training and no experience – which was the root cause of their ultimate fate.

Unlike the Japanese battleships of Togo's First Division, which spent the entire war under his inspired leadership, the Russian battleships of the Pacific Squadron were led by four different senior officers between February and December 1904. In just ten months, the Pacific Squadron was commanded by Stark, Makarov, Vitgeft and Viren, with two of them killed in action and one relieved of command. This steady succession of leaders, with constant shifts between passive and aggressive leadership, greatly undermined the effectiveness of the Pacific Squadron. While the 2nd Pacific Squadron served its entire eight-month career under Vice-Adm Rozhestvensky, his acerbic leadership style prevented the formation of any team spirit among the crews.

Indeed, Rozhestvensky's rapid promotion to fleet commander and the manner in which he achieved it was indicative of the rot in the Tsarist fleet. Two years before the war,

---

6    Formed in 1810, this Naval Infantry battalion distinguished itself at Borodino in 1812. Both officers and enlisted members of the battalion formed the crews and guards on the Tsar's Imperial yachts.

# CAPTAIN EDUARD N. SHCHENSNOVICH (1852–1910)

Shchensnovich was born in Arkhangelsk. He came from a noble family, and his father was a naval officer. Graduating from the Naval Academy in 1871, he earned a reputation during service in the Baltic as a specialist in mine warfare. In 1885 he was sent to the Pacific to organize the first torpedo boat units at Vladivostok. Returning to the Baltic, he commanded a coastal defense battleship, and then a cruiser. In late 1898, he was sent to Philadelphia to supervise the construction of the new battleship *Retvizan* and took command when it was commissioned in 1902. During the Battle of the Yellow Sea in August 1904, Shchensnovich boldly charged Togo's battle line – a move that saved the Russian flagship, but which resulted in his being badly wounded in the stomach by shrapnel. After the fall of Port Arthur and his repatriation to Russia, he was promoted to Rear Admiral, and in 1906 the Tsar put him in charge of organizing Russia's first operational submarine squadron at Libau. Shchensnovich was instrumental in helping to rebuild the Russian Navy after the disasters of the Russo-Japanese War and he wrote extensively on mine warfare and submarines as cheaper alternatives for the defense of Russia's coastline. However, he never fully recovered from his wounds and shortly after being promoted to Vice-Admiral, he died in April 1910.

Captain Eduard N. Shchensnovich (Author's collection)

# CAPTAIN NIKOLAI M. YAKOVLEV (1856–1919)

Yakovlev was from the nobility in Nikolyaev and he graduated from the Naval Academy in 1876. He specialized in navigation and served in that role in the Russo-Turkish War in 1877, and then became a staff officer in the Pacific Squadron in 1891. After serving on several gunboats and cruisers in the 1890s, Yakovlev was promoted to Captain 1st Rank in 1901 and given command of the battleship *Petropavlovsk* in 1902. Yakovlev was very fortunate to survive the sinking of *Petropavlovsk* on April 13, 1904, bu he was badly wounded and was sent back to recover in Europe before Port Arthur was isolated. Back in St Petersburg, Yakovlev put his experience from the Far East to use in supervising the construction of the new battleship *Imperator Pavel I*. Thereafter, Yakovlev was promoted to Vice-Admiral in 1909 and Admiral in 1915, serving on the Admiralty Council. Like many Tsarist naval officers, Yakovlev fell foul of the Cheka after the Bolshevik Revolution and he was executed in 1919.

Captain Nikolai M. Yakovlev (Author's collection)

Rozhestvensky had been captain of the elderly cruiser *Minin*, a gunnery training ship in the Baltic. On July 24 1902, the *Minin* was tasked with putting on a gunnery demonstration at Reval (Tallinn) for Tsar Nicholas II and the visiting Kaiser Wilhelm II. Rozhestvensky put on a spectacular "dog and pony" show for the monarchs, appearing to hit virtually all the stationary and moving targets with a handpicked gun crew. The visibly pleased Tsar, who had a fatal tendency toward favoritism and picking the wrong man for the job, marked Rozhestvensky for rapid promotion to flag rank. Despite the fact that the gunnery exercise had no relation to actual combat conditions, the Tsar believed Rozhestvensky to be a "gunnery expert" and well suited to command a fleet.

## THE JAPANESE BATTLESHIP CREW

Japanese battleship crews ranged from 637 in the *Fuji*-class to 773 on the *Asahi*, including about 50–60 officers. About half of the crew – around 350 men – was involved in operating and supplying the ship's armament. Each 12-in gun had 11 men in the turret, 12 in the shell room and 20 in the magazine. The large number of light quick-firing guns also required robust ammunition parties to resupply the weapons from below-deck magazines. The engine room crew comprised the other major component of the crew, with up to 200 stokers, engineers and mechanics operating the power plant. The remainder of the crew included signalmen, lookouts, medical personnel and bridge personnel.

A Japanese signalman and officer next to a 12-pounder (76.2mm) gun mount. Japanese battleship crews were trained to function as a team and although discipline was strict, morale was high. (Museum of Fine Arts, Boston)

Enlisted sailors in the IJN consisted of both conscripts and volunteers. The conscripts were drafted for a period of eight years, followed by four more years in the reserves. Sailors were initially trained at the three main naval bases, Yokosuka, Kure and Sasebo. Many sailors came from small coastal communities in the southern Japanese provinces and were accustomed both to hard work and the sea. Despite coming from rural backgrounds, virtually all the IJN sailors were literate, which greatly facilitated training. However, sailors were discouraged from reading newspapers that might contain socialist or radical viewpoints; the IJN wanted to ensure their sailors were not distracted from their duty by a swirl of competing ideas. Since Japanese culture idealized military duty and service to the Emperor, there were numerous volunteer sailors who joined the navy for patriotic reasons. In addition to high morale and patriotism, Japanese battleship sailors were paid double the rate of their army counterparts and were well fed. Furthermore, they were treated with respect by their officers, and hard-working enlisted men could hope for promotion to the NCO ranks.

Naval officers were trained at the Imperial Japanese Naval Academy (*Kaigun Heigakkō*), located at Etajima near Hiroshima since 1888. A British training mission had arrived in 1873 to establish the academy and the high standards for officer training. Admission to Etajima was very strict, with only 183 out of 2,326 applicants admitted in 1904. Until 1898 class sizes were kept small, but by 1899–1900 the rapid expansion of the IJN required the academy to triple its output. Cadets spent four years in training and then went on long overseas cruises. Japanese naval officers received a fairly technical education but they were also imbued with the "Nelson tradition" through their British advisors, which instilled tactical aggressiveness. Interestingly, the officers ranked highest in their class usually followed a staff or technical path, while all the future battleship officers were in the bottom half of their class at the academy.

The seven men who commanded Japan's battleships in 1904–05 were an extremely homogenous group; all were graduates of the Naval Academy between 1875 and 1878 and at the start of the war they were aged between 44 and 49. Of these seven officers, five were from southern Japan. The IJN wanted its officers to be well rounded, experienced in a variety of areas; thus in addition to considerable time ashore as staff officers, four had been naval attachés and four had been instructors at the Naval Academy. Since the IJN needed to learn from foreign navies it emphasized overseas duty for its best officers to expose them to new naval technologies and tactics. Capt Nomoto Tsunaakira, commander of the *Asahi* in 1904, was sent to St Petersburg as the Japanese naval attaché twice, in 1893–95 and 1898–1901. Before getting a battleship command, these seven officers each had two to five prior commands for a total of 22–52 months each. Interestingly all six Japanese battleships received new commanders in the period June–November 1903, indicating a premeditated preparation for war.

Japanese battleship crews were intensely trained, particularly in gunnery. Since Japan was still a poor country, it could not afford to expend great amounts of ammunition on training or to replace worn-out gun barrels, so it became one of the first navies to enthusiastically embrace the use of simulators and sub-caliber devices. During gunnery training, spotting rifles were mounted inside the barrels of 12-in guns and linked to the standard electric firing switches, enabling the gun crew to engage targets out to about 1.8km. While the range of sub-caliber target practice was much less than actual combat, it allowed gun crews to repeatedly practice laying on targets and engaging them quickly. Before the war, the *Mikasa* annually fired 29,000 sub-caliber rounds, but prior to Tsushima the ship fired 30,000 sub-caliber rounds in only ten days of training. Japanese gunnery officers also trained extensively with their new Barr & Stroud FA3 rangefinders. However, the Japanese could not afford to expend much ammunition on long-range gunnery training, so they were much less prepared for the type of long-range engagements that occurred in the two main battleship actions of the Russo-Japanese War. Due to this intensive training, Japanese battleships had about twice the rate of fire of Russian battleships, although their accuracy beyond 5km was no better than that of the Russians.

## CAPTAIN SAKAMOTO HAJIME (1859–1948)

Captain Sakamoto Hajime commanded the battleship *Yashima* from October 1903. He was from Kochi and entered the Naval Academy in October 1874, graduating 28th out of 30 in Class 7. Sakamoto served on the cruiser *Tsukuba* in 1879–84, and then *Naniwa* in 1885–86. After a stint as an instructor at Naval Academy in 1886–87, he returned to sea duty on cruisers in 1890–94. In the Sino-Japanese War, he distinguished himself on the gunboat *Akagi* at the Battle of the Yalu in September 1894. After the war, he was assigned to the new battleship *Fuji* as chief navigator in 1896–98, then XO of *Yashima* for eight months in 1898. He was given his first command in 1899 and promoted to captain in 1900, commanding two cruisers in 1901–02. After the loss of his ship, Sakamoto was put in charge of the vital supply port at Darien in late 1904 and was then given command of the battleship *Fuji* in late 1905. In December 1905 he traveled to England to take command of the new battleship *Katori*, one of the last built overseas. Sakamoto was promoted to Rear Admiral in 1907 and Vice-Admiral in 1908, finishing his successful navy career on the Admiralty Committee at the start of World War I.

Captain Sakamoto Hajime (Museum of Fine Arts, Boston)

## REAR ADMIRAL NASHIBA TOKIOKI (1850–1928)

Commanding the battleship sub-division in Togo's 1st Division, Nashiba was born in Yamaguchi. He did not enter the Imperial Japanese Navy directly, but served first in the Ministry of the Interior and only transferred in 1880 at the age of 30. He served virtually all of the 1880s on training ships and became the chief trainer at the Navy Academy in 1891. Nashiba then went through no fewer than nine commands between 1894 and 1901, beginning with gunboats, working up to cruisers and culminating in command of the battleship *Hatsuse* in 1901–02. Nashiba was promoted to Rear Admiral in 1903 and given command of the Kure naval yard. During the Russo-Japanese War, Nashiba barely survived the sinking of the *Yashima* in April 1904 and his performance during the operations around Port Arthur was mediocre. After the war, Nashiba was made a baron and promoted to Vice-Admiral, but he never held any more important commands.

Rear Admiral Nashiba Tokioki (Museum of Fine Arts, Boston)

# COMBAT

## OPENING ACTION AT PORT ARTHUR
## FEBRUARY 8–9, 1904

On February 5, Togo received his orders to commence hostilities against Russia. Although Japan severed diplomatic relations on February 6, 1904, the Tsar directed that Russian forces were not to fire the first shots so that Japan would appear the aggressor. Admiral Stark was concerned that his battleships might be trapped in the inner harbor in case of a sudden Japanese attack, so he decided to keep his squadron of seven battleships and seven cruisers anchored in the roadstead outside Port Arthur. The fleet was anchored in three lines parallel to the coast: five battleships were in the inner row; the *Tsesarevich, Retvizan* and three cruisers were in the middle row; and four cruisers were in the outer row. Two Russian destroyers patrolled about 30km outside the port. By remaining in the roadstead, the fleet could sortie fairly quickly, but this deployment required a level of vigilance that Stark failed to enforce. Stark did order his battleship captains to deploy their anti-torpedo nets but he was ignored and his staff failed to correct this omission. Furthermore, protective minefields around the roadstead had not been laid and the coastal batteries were not fully operational or manned.

Japanese warships bombarding Port Arthur. The initial clash between Russian and Japanese battleships was indecisive and the gunnery quite poor. (Museum of Fine Arts, Boston)

Vice-Adm Togo intended to achieve a knockout blow at the start of the war with a daring nighttime torpedo boat attack, to be possibly followed by a daylight bombardment from all six Japanese battleships. At dusk on February 8, Togo's fleet of six battleships, nine cruisers and 11 destroyers moved to within striking range of Port Arthur. At 1900 hours, Togo released three destroyer divisions with ten boats to attack the Russian fleet, but less than two hours later they were spotted by the Russian picket destroyers. The Japanese destroyers evaded the picket ships but the attack group lost cohesion in the dark, and only four were able to take part in the initial torpedo attack at 2350 hours. Seven 18-in torpedoes were fired at ranges of 400–600m against stationary targets, yet only one hit the battleship *Retvizan* on the bow and another hit the protected cruiser *Pallada*. The Japanese destroyers sped off, unharmed. Despite the obvious beginning of hostilities, the Russians milled around in confusion until the other six Japanese destroyers finally arrived two hours later. Searchlights and small-caliber guns did come into action against the second attack, which forced the Japanese destroyers to launch from 1.5km. Of the twelve torpedoes launched in the second attack, one hit the *Tsesarevich* near the stern.

Of the seven Russian battleships, only two had been hit. The *Retvizan* had a large hole near her bow that let in 2,200 tons of water, causing an 11° list, but power was soon restored and only five crewmen were killed. The *Tsesarevich* had an 18° list but was soon able to move toward the inner harbor with the aid of tugboats. Both damaged battleships grounded near the shallow harbor entrance, but they were in no danger of sinking and their armament and crews were intact. Togo had made a serious mistake with the destroyer attack in failing to provide at least one ship with a radio to inform him of the results. This mistake was compounded when a reconnaissance outside Port Arthur by Japanese cruisers at 0800 hours incorrectly reported to Togo that the Russian fleet was still milling around in confusion due to the torpedo attack and was vulnerable. In fact, the Russian fleet had recovered from the initial shock and the five undamaged battleships all had steam up and the defenses were now fully alert.

The battleship *Pobieda* limps into Port Arthur after being mined, following the Battle of the Yellow Sea. Aside from the unfortunate *Petropavlovsk*, Russian battleships repeatedly demonstrated an ability to survive underwater damage. (Naval Historical Center, NH100045)

Ten hours after the torpedo attack ended, Togo's fleet approached Port Arthur from the south-east with six battleships, five armored cruisers and four protected cruisers. Togo hoped to deliver the *coup de grâce* to the Russian battleships before they could recover their wits. Instead, the fleet was spotted by the cruiser *Boyarin* on patrol, which fled and alerted the rest of the Russian squadron. Out in front, Togo's flagship *Mikasa* came within sight of Port Arthur by 1110 hours and was fired upon by the 10-in Coastal Battery No. 15 on Electric Hill, which had five modern 10-in/45-caliber M1892 guns mounted in cement barbettes. Two other Russian coastal batteries were also operational that morning – No. 9 on the Tiger Tail Peninsula with five 6-in/45-caliber Canét M1892 guns and No. 12 on Golden Hill with six elderly 11-in guns. Lookouts on the *Mikasa* spotted the Russian fleet, with *Tsesarevich* and *Retvizan* grounded near the harbor mouth, but the other five battleships and six cruisers moving slowly to the west in three parallel columns along the coast. Although suspecting that the earlier report was inaccurate, Togo rashly decided to simultaneously attack the shore batteries and the Russian fleet. *Mikasa* altered course to port, heading west toward the Russian squadron, but Togo decided to engage the coastal batteries with his 12-in guns while his 6-in guns engaged the Russian fleet. At noon, *Mikasa* fired a 12-in ranging shot from a range of 8km and soon every ship on both sides was firing. The shore batteries – which were more accurate as they did not have to correct for pitch or roll – soon

got *Mikasa*'s range and hit her with two 10-in shells. The Russian fire from both the coastal batteries and battleships became increasingly accurate as the range to target dropped to about 6km and soon *Fuji* was hit on the forward bridge by a large-caliber round. *Hatsuse* was hit twice and *Shikishima* was hit by a 6-in shell. Three Japanese cruisers were also damaged. On the Russian side, the *Petropavlovsk*, *Pobeda*, *Poltava*, *Sevastopol* and

The cruiser *Pallada* (left) and battleship *Pobieda* (right) under fire inside the inner basin of Port Arthur. Although Japanese efforts to engage the Russian squadron with long-range gunnery failed to sink any warships, it did inflict damage on a regular basis. (Library of Congress) NH100045)

### Damage to battleships in action off Port Arthur, February 9, 1904

| Name | Hits | Casualties |
|---|---|---|
| Petropavlovsk | Hit on bow, probably by two 12-in and one 6-in | 2 killed, 5 wounded |
| Pobieda | Hit amidships near waterline | 2 killed, 4 wounded |
| Poltava | Hit twice on aft hull | |
| Sevastopol | Hit on upper forward deck by 6- or 8-in shell | 2 wounded |
| Mikasa | Hit twice by 10-in shells | 7 wounded |
| Fuji | Hit by large shell on forward bridge and 75mm shell on aft conning tower | 2 killed, 10 wounded |
| Hatsuse | Hit twice | 7 killed, 17 wounded |
| Shikishima | Hit by 6-in shell | 17 wounded |

four cruisers were hit, mostly by 6-in and 8-in rounds that did not penetrate. By 1220 hours, Togo had had enough of this punishment and realized that he could not fight both the fleet and shore batteries, so he ordered a turn to the south away from Port Arthur.

The battleship action off Port Arthur was a minor Russian tactical victory since the Japanese fleet had been driven off after making only a single pass. Togo had erred badly in committing his battleships to a major action with inadequate reconnaissance and in risking his precious capital ships against alerted shore batteries. By splitting his fire between shore batteries and enemy warships, Togo allowed the Russian battleships to achieve firepower superiority despite their lower rate of fire. As a result, four of his six battleships were hit, suffering 60 casualties, while four of the seven Russian battleships were hit by smaller-caliber shells, which caused only 17 casualties. Instead, the Japanese concentrated fire on the cruiser *Bayan*, which was hit nine times including by two 12-in rounds. An additional twenty 12-in rounds landed in the town of Port Arthur, demonstrating the poor accuracy of Japanese gunnery in this action.

Following Togo's failure to cripple the Russian battleship fleet at Port Arthur, he tried several daring efforts to close the narrow harbor mouth with blockships but these raids were also failures. Meanwhile, the Russian Naval Ministry reacted to the surprise attack on Port Arthur by relieving Vice-Adm Stark. On March 7, 1904, Vice-Adm Stepan O. Makarov, hero of the Russo-Turkish War, arrived in Port Arthur to take command of the Pacific Squadron. Makarov also brought the skilled engineer Nikolai E. Kuteinikov and a team of repair experts, who were assigned to fix the *Retvizan* and *Tsesarevich*. Makarov himself was a dynamic, aggressive commander who immediately took steps to improve the morale and effectiveness of the fleet. In his initial meeting with his ships' captains, Makarov told them that he intended to keep the fleet intact until reinforcements from the Baltic could arrive, but that the squadron would operate outside the protected area of the fortress in order to gain experience and to keep the Japanese off-balance. Instead of lurking behind costal defenses and minefields, Makarov pushed the fleet out to make aggressive sorties to harass the loose Japanese blockade, which mostly consisted of cruisers and destroyers. Togo's battleships remained in distant support, about 110km to the east near the Elliot Islands. The result of Makarov's new command style was a series of small-scale naval skirmishes in March in the waters around Port Arthur.

Having failed to blockade the harbor, Togo tried a new tactic to get at the Russian battleships in Port Arthur. On March 22 he sent Rear Adm Nashiba's sub-division with the battleships *Fuji* and *Yashima* to Pigeon Bay, on the south-west side of the Liaodung Peninsula, where they could not be seen by Russian coastal batteries. Although Nashiba's battleships could not see into Port Arthur due to intervening hills, they fired 154 12-in rounds at the extreme range of 9.5km in the general direction of the inner harbor. Meanwhile, the Russians had finally gotten the damaged *Retvizan* off the sandbar near the entrance and moved it to the eastern basin, where Kuteinikov's engineers built a wooden cofferdam around the torpedo hole in its side. As shells fell randomly into the harbor area a repair crew on the *Retvizan* continued to pump out the ship's flooded compartments, but at around 1100 hours one of the Japanese 12-in shells hit its port side. Incredibly, the shell hit near the torpedo hole and smashed both the cofferdam and drainage hoses, causing further flooding. *Retvizan*'s bow was soon nearly underwater, and the crew suffered five dead and ten wounded in the attack. Also hit was the battleship *Tsesarevich*, which was also under repair.

Makarov was incensed by this Japanese tactic and he took immediate measures to prevent a repetition. Four 6-in guns were removed from the *Retvizan* and installed on a hill overlooking Pigeon Bay. An observation post with a telephone link back to the fleet was also installed on another hilltop. Nashiba's sub-division returned on March 22 but the *Fuji* and *Yashima* had just begun to fire when they started receiving return fire from the harbor area. The *Retvizan* and *Pobeda* were firing from the Western Basin and receiving corrections from the Russian observation post. After several salvoes, *Retvizan* was able to score a 12-in hit on the *Fuji*, which quickly departed the area. The two *Peresvyet*-class battleships were particularly well suited for this type of long-range gunnery duel since they could elevate their 10-in guns to 35° against only 15° for all of the other battleships. A few weeks later Togo tried to use his faster armored cruisers to try "shoot-n-scoot" type tactics into the harbor, but the *Peresvyet* scored a 10-in hit on his cruiser *Nisshin*.

Since both blockships and bombardment had failed to neutralize the Russian battleships, Togo decided to try and use mines to seal off Port Arthur. On the night of April 12, a Japanese minelayer laid 48 contact mines in two fields off the east and west approaches to the harbor mouth. The next morning, a skirmish between Russian and Japanese destroyers provoked Makarov into a sortie with his flagship *Petropavlovsk* and *Poltava*. At 0715 hours on April 13, Makarov steamed out of the harbor with his two battleships and four cruisers. The Japanese cruisers fired a few shots and then turned away at 0810 hours, as Makarov's ships approached. Makarov's pursuit brought him some 24km away from Port Arthur when suddenly Togo's five battleships appeared out of the early morning mist at 0840 hours. With only two battleships against five, Makarov turned about and headed back toward the rest of his fleet and the safety of Port Arthur's coastal batteries. Although *Mikasa* was able to close the distance to the rearmost Russian ships to only 6.9km in just half an hour, Togo broke off the pursuit at 0930 hours when his ships began to come within range of the coastal batteries.

Thirteen minutes later, just as Makarov's ships appeared to have reached safety, the *Petropavlovsk* struck a mine[7] at 0943 hours. Captain Vladimir Semenoff, on the cruiser *Diana*, described what he saw:

> I went on the forecastle, where I stood at the starboard bow 6-inch gun, and was just giving the boatswain the usual orders, when an explosion, with a dull, rolling sound shook the whole ship, as if a 12-inch gun had gone off quite close. I looked round vaguely. A second explosion, even more violent! What was happening? Suddenly cries of horror arose: "The *Petropavlovsk*! The *Petropavlovsk*!" Dreading the worst, I rushed to the side. I saw a huge cloud of brown smoke. In this cloud I saw the ship's foremast. It was slanting, helpless, not as if it was falling, but as if it were suspended in the air. To the left of this cloud I saw the battleship's stern. It looked as always, as if the awful happenings in the fore-part were none of its concern. A third explosion! White steam now began to mix with the brown cloud. The boilers had burst! Suddenly the stern of the battleship rose straight in the air. This happened so rapidly that it did not look as if the bow had gone down, but as if the ship had broken in half amidships. For a moment I saw the screws whirling round in the air. Was there a further explosion? I don't know. It appeared to me as if the after-part of the *Petropavlovsk* (all that was visible of her) suddenly opened out and belched forth fire and flames, like a volcano. It seemed even as if flames came out of the sea, long after it had closed over the wreck."[8]

The *Petropavlovsk* sank in less than two minutes, taking with it Vice-Adm Makarov, the squadron gunnery officer Capt Aleksandr K. Miakishev and 677 members of her crew.

---

7   The Japanese used conical contact mines with a 100kg charge of wet gun cotton and a maximum depth of 330 feet.

8   Semenoff, *Rasplata*.

her crew. Later investigation concluded that the contact mine probably detonated one of the *Petropavlovsk*'s forward-mounted torpedoes, which triggered a sympathetic detonation of a store of 50 mines, then the 12-in ammunition magazine. After picking up the 80-odd survivors, the stunned Russian squadron headed back to the harbor when the *Pobieda* also hit a mine at 1015 hours. Fortunately, the *Pobieda* was hit amidships and although it took on an 11° list, it was able to make it into the port under its own power. With Stark relieved, Makarov dead and three of its six remaining battleships incapacitated, morale in the Pacific Squadron plummeted.

Rear Adm Vilgelm K. Vitgeft was appointed the new commander of the 1st Pacific Squadron[9] after Makarov's death, but he was a staff officer unsuited for senior leadership and he reverted to a passive policy. However, Vitgeft's preference for a "fleet-in-being" approach was more consistent with Russia's naval strategy than Makarov's "bull-in-a-china-shop" approach that resulted in heavy operational losses. When the Japanese 2nd Army landed on the Liaodung Peninsula 96km north-east of Port Arthur on May 5, Vitgeft's battleships sat immobile in the inner harbor. Five days later the Japanese cut off Port Arthur's rail line and the base was now isolated.

Emboldened by the inactivity of the Russian battleships, Togo decided to resume routine bombardments of Port Arthur by mixed battleship-cruiser squadrons. In response, Vitgeft increased the mining effort begun by Makarov. On the morning of May 15, it was Rear Adm Nashiba's turn with the battleships *Yashima*, *Hatsuse* and *Shikishima* to bombard the harbor. Nashiba's task force approached within 16km of the harbor when it steamed right into a new Russian minefield.[10] *Hatsuse* was struck first at 1050 hours and its steering and engines were disabled, leaving it adrift. Maneuvering to clear the disabled *Hatsuse*, *Yashima* struck a mine too. As escort ships closed in to assist, the *Hatsuse* drifted onto another mine, which detonated one of the forward magazines, causing her to sink in about 90 seconds. Although the escorts managed to rescue Nashiba, Capt Nakao and 334 members of the crew, 496 men went down with the ship. Russian observers near Port Arthur spotted the destruction of the *Hatsuse*, but could not determine the extent of damage to the *Yashima*, which was towed out of the area. The Japanese were able to get *Yashima* away from Port Arthur but they could not control its flooding and by the time the ship approached Encounter Rock at around 1700 hours it was clearly sinking. Capt Sakamoto assembled the entire crew on the deck of the doomed battleship and together sang the national anthem *Kimi-ga-yo*, then gave three

Port Arthur viewed from the top of 203-Meter Hill. The distance to the Russian battleships in the distance is 5,700 meters. (Author's collection)

9   The Pacific Squadron was renamed on April 17, 1904.
10  The Russian Model 1898 moored contact mine had a 56kg charge of wet gun cotton and could be placed to a maximum depth of 400 feet.

*Banzais* and took to the lifeboats. Three hours later, the *Yashima* capsized and sank. Togo's impatience to get at the Russian battleships had played right into the hands of the Russian Navy's attrition strategy and cost him one-third of his battleship division. Furthermore, the success of the Russian cruiser squadron from Vladivostok in harassing Japan's shipping caused Togo to send Adm Kamimura's armored cruisers to the Sea of Japan, which further reduced Togo's ability to form a sufficiently strong battle line to counter the Russian squadron in Port Arthur.

The naval balance changed even more sharply in early June as the dockyard in Port Arthur finished repairs on the *Retvizan*, *Tsesarevich* and *Pobieda*. Vitgeft now had six operational battleships against Togo's four, but he was reluctant to risk them in the mine-infested waters outside the harbor. After much prodding by his superiors, Vitgeft was persuaded to sortie the 1st Pacific Squadron on June 23 with the intention of reaching Vladivostok, where the fleet could operate with greater freedom of action. Vitgeft sailed at 1630 hours with six battleships, five cruisers and seven destroyers. Around 1800 hours, the Russian squadron spotted Togo's squadron, which had four battleships, six cruisers and about 30 destroyers and torpedo boats. Togo was surprised to see that the Russians had repaired their three damaged battleships and he was reluctant to engage a superior number of enemy capital ships. By 1845 hours, Togo's squadron was moving parallel to the Russian squadron, but beyond effective firing range, at a distance of about 13km. At this point, with sunset approaching and the Japanese fleet outnumbered in terms of heavy guns, Vitgeft had the edge and he stood an excellent chance of fighting a brief running action until he could escape to Vladivostok under cover of darkness. Realizing that he could not allow the Russian squadron to escape without a fight, Togo gradually began to close the distance with the intention of beginning a long-range gunnery duel. But Vitgeft had no stomach for a fight and at 1900 hours he turned his flagship *Tsesarevich* around and led the fleet back toward Port Arthur. Seeing the Russians retreat, Togo decided to conserve his battleships but released his destroyers to conduct torpedo attacks on the rear ships in the Russian squadron. The Japanese destroyers harried Vitgeft all the way back to Port Arthur but scored no hits. However, on the way back to Port Arthur, the *Sevastopol* hit a mine, causing 11 casualties and severe flooding, but the ship was able to make it back to the roadstead. Vitgeft's best chance for escaping to Vladivostok had been thrown away.

A Japanese 11-in siege howitzer shells the Russian battleships in Port Arthur. Crude Russian efforts to protect the wooden decks of their battleships by laying sections of extra steel plate atop their vulnerable areas proved futile and the plunging fire of the Japanese guns inflicted far more damage than Togo's flat-trajectory 12-in shells had achieved at the Yellow Sea. (Author's collection)

# THE BATTLE OF THE YELLOW SEA
# AUGUST 10, 1904

Vitgeft was now content to remain safe in harbor until the expected reinforcements from the Baltic arrived later in the year, but events on the ground interfered. By early August 1904, the Japanese 3rd Army was approaching the outer ground defenses of

Port Arthur. Once within artillery range, the Japanese Naval Brigade brought up two 4.7-in howitzers and began to shell the harbor areas on August 7. The flagship *Tsesarevich* was hit twice and by chance, a shell fragment wounded Vitgeft in the leg, literally stinging him into action. Two days later, another bombardment at 0755 hours hit the battleship *Retvizan* seven times and one 4.7-in shell struck below the armored belt, flooding five compartments. Capt Eduard Shchensnovich was also wounded by one of the shells. Clearly, the days of the fleet sitting snugly in harbor awaiting support were over. A message arrived from the Tsar, ordering Vitgeft to take the fleet to Vladivostok immediately. Vitgeft felt that he was a lamb being pushed to the slaughter and gave one of the least inspiring pre-battle speeches in history, telling his officers, "Gentlemen, we shall meet in the next world."

All the Russian battleships, including the damaged *Retvizan*, began leaving the inner harbor at 0615 hours and waited while small craft swept for mines in the approaches to Port Arthur. At 0955 hours, Vitgeft sailed out of the anchorage with six battleships, three cruisers and eight destroyers. Oddly, he allowed the hospital ship *Mongolia* to tag along behind his squadron. Furthermore, it was a clear day, and several nearby Japanese cruisers on blockade duty promptly radioed Togo about the departure of the Russian ships. Yet the Russian naval sortie caught Togo's naval forces dispersed, with Togo's four battleships 60km south of Port Arthur near Round Island, Vice-Adm Dewa's cruisers to the west and other cruisers and destroyers to the east, supporting the Japanese ground campaign at Port Arthur. Vitgeft was cunning enough to steer toward the south-west first – rather than heading directly for the open sea – which made it difficult for Togo to determine his course of action. Uncertain as to Vitgeft's intent, Togo delayed concentrating his fleet, although he had already given a previous order for all units to assemble near Encounter Rock in the event of a Russian escape attempt. By 1100 hours it was clear from Japanese ships shadowing Vitgeft's squadron that the Russians were making for the open sea. Togo started moving his forces, hoping to cut off the Russian escape.

Vitgeft's squadron was not in the best of shape since two of his ships still had damage from artillery fire and a number of ships were suffering from mechanical difficulties. Both *Tsesarevich* and *Pobeda* developed engine defects within an hour of leaving port that caused the fleet to slow down. Furthermore, the fleet did not have its full armament since *Sevastopol* had one inoperative 12-in gun in its aft turret and a total of 11 6-in, 10 75mm, seven 47mm and 16 37mm guns had been stripped from the battleships and sent to bolster Port Arthur's land defenses. Vitgeft led the squadron in the *Tsesarevich*, followed by the *Retvizan*, *Pobeda*, *Peresvyet*, *Sevastopol*, *Poltava* and three protected cruisers. The cruiser *Novik* led eight destroyers in a separate column on the port beam of the main column.

At 1225 hours, both battle fleets sighted each other south of Encounter Rock at a distance of about 19km, with Vitgeft steaming south-east at 13 knots and Togo approaching on an intercept course from the north-east at 14 knots. Togo was in the lead with *Mikasa*, followed by the *Asahi*, *Fuji*, *Shikishima* and the armored cruisers *Kasuga* and *Nisshin*. Due to the loss of *Hatsuse* and *Yashima*, Togo had decided to add *Nisshin* and *Kasuga* into his main battle line to compensate for the superior number of enemy battleships. The *Kasuga*-class cruisers were powerful warships that packed 8-in and 10-in guns and up to 6ins of armored protection, but they lacked the

# BATTLE OF YELLOW SEA
## TOGO'S STERN CHASE, AUGUST 10, 1904, 1445–1505 HOURS

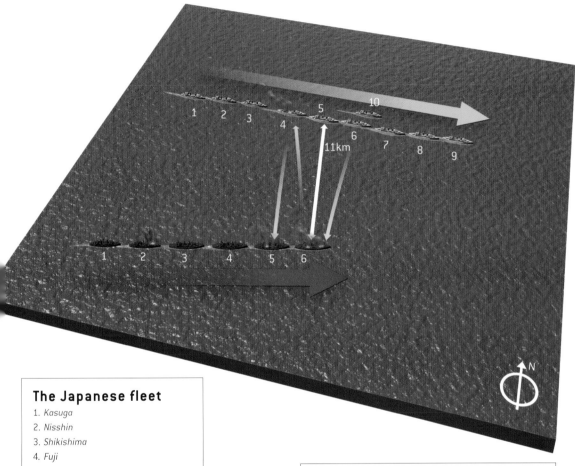

## The Japanese fleet

1. *Kasuga*
2. *Nisshin*
3. *Shikishima*
4. *Fuji*
5. *Asahi*
6. *Mikasa* commanded by Admiral Togo

## The Russian fleet accompanied by a group of eight destroyers.

1. The cruiser *Pallada*
2. The cruiser *Diana*
3. The cruiser *Askold*
4. The cruiser *Poltava*
5. The battleship *Sevastopol*
6. The battleship *Peresvyet*, commanded by Prince Ukhtomski
7. The battleship *Pobeda*
8. The battleship *Retvizan*
9. The battleship *Tsesarevich*, commanded by Admiral Vitgeft
10. The cruiser *Novik*

Togo's battleships are pursuing Vitgeft's battlefleet, which has succeeded in slipping past him. Both fleets are moving eastwards at 14 knots, while Togo's battleships have closed to within 11,000 meters of the rearmost Russian battleship, the *Poltava*. However, Prince Ukhtomski orders his entire sub-division to concentrate on the two lead Japanese battleships and both *Mikasa* and *Asahi* are damaged.

## Key

General direction of Japanese Fleet Divisions →
Line of escape of Russian Fleet →
Lines of fire →
Direct hit on a ship

49

survivability of battleships. Also within sight were Vice-Adm Dewa's four cruisers, approaching from the south at 18 knots. It appeared that the Russian fleet could be squeezed between the two oncoming Japanese columns.

Shortly after 1300 hours, Togo tried to "cross the T" on the approaching Russians and *Mikasa* opened the action by firing a few ranging shots at *Tsesarevich* at the extreme range of 13km. *Tsesarevich* and *Retvizan* returned the fire, but the range was too extreme and neither side scored any hits. Togo miscalculated early in the action – he should have reduced his speed so as to allow the Russians to get closer before he attempted to "cross the T." Instead, Vitgeft turned to port; increasing the range and heading past the tail of Togo's column. In minutes, both fleets were heading on opposite courses, with Vitgeft having a clear path to the open sea. Not only did Togo fail to block Vitgeft's path, but his course also caused Dewa to turn his four cruisers away without firing a shot so as to avoid interfering with the main Japanese battle line. The favorable initial Japanese position had been squandered.

Seeing the Russian battle line heading past the rear of his battle line at 14 knots, Togo ordered each ship to turn individually to the east and ended up with his cruisers in the lead. At 1325 hours, Togo's division was now on a roughly parallel course with Vitgeft's squadron and the Japanese battleships opened fire at the extreme range of 13km, concentrating on the *Tsesarevich* and *Retvizan*. The *Retvizan* was hit 12 times, but only one hit caused serious damage. Vitgeft's battleships returned fire and the Russian accuracy at this range was quite good: *Mikasa* was hit twice by 12-in shells between 1333 and 1337 hours, disabling her wireless and damaging the mainmast. Both battle lines pounded each other with 12-in and 10-in shells for about 20 minutes in a long-range gunnery duel, as the range steadily dropped. By 1405 hours, the range had dropped to less than 8km and the 6-in guns on both sides began to join in. Although Togo's ships began firing full salvoes, he opted to turn away slightly at this point, due to the damage his flagship was taking. Simultaneously, Togo was

The battleship *Tsesarevich* after the Battle of the Yellow Sea. Despite being hit by 15 12-in shells, the *Tsesarevich* escaped from its Japanese pursuers. This photo clearly shows the tumblehome shape of the hull and how this squat shape provided ample waterline protection. (Naval Historical Center, NH60709)

frantically trying to get Dewa's cruisers to re-engage the Russian van and for Rear Adm Togo to close with his three cruisers from the north, but the early loss of his radio greatly reduced his ability to exploit his superior numbers. Instead, Togo had to signal his orders to the *Asahi* behind his flagship, and then it used its radio to relay his orders, resulting in lengthy delays.

Both battle fleets were now making 14 knots and due to his maneuvers, Togo had allowed Vitgeft to get past him. Togo began a stern chase, only able to use his bow and portside guns. The Russian battleships had fired a few 12-in rounds at Dewa's and Togo's cruisers, driving them off, so the Japanese superiority in numbers had come to naught. By 1445 hours, the *Mikasa* had closed to within about 11km of the trail Russian battleship, the *Poltava*, which was unable to maintain 14 knots due to engine problems. Togo concentrated the fire of his lead ships on *Poltava* and soon scored several hits. However, Prince Ukhtomski slowed his division to support the *Poltava* and the Russian battleships concentrated on *Mikasa* and *Asahi*. The *Asahi* was hit first at 1450 hours, then *Mikasa* at 1500 hours and again at 1505 hours. As the Japanese closed to within 8.5km of the tail end of the Russian column, the *Poltava* scored two more 12-in hits on the *Mikasa* and one on the *Nisshin*. Togo's chief of staff urged him to back off and use his superior speed to get ahead of the Russians, so he turned to starboard to increase the range. By 1520 hours, firing ceased as the range opened.

Just as the main action died down, Dewa finally decided to get his cruisers into the battle, but the Russian battleships then shifted their fire onto his small squadron. At 1540 hours a 12-in round struck Dewa's flagship, the *Yakumo*, at a range of over 13km – beyond the range of his 8-in guns. Dewa decided that it was foolish for four lightly armored cruisers to get closer to six enemy battleships so he wisely broke off the action and turned away from Vitgeft. Russian gunfire also drove off Rear Adm Togo's three cruisers, so Togo's four battleships and two cruisers were the only Japanese units actively chasing Vitgeft's six battleships and four cruisers. This would have been an opportune moment for Vitgeft to turn to starboard and pound Togo's forward ships, particularly the more vulnerable armored cruisers. Instead, Vitgeft stuck doggedly to his course, sensing that he had made it past Togo and could lose him once darkness fell in three hours.

Togo realized that that battle was going against him – the Russian fleet was escaping and night was approaching – so he increased speed to 15 knots in order to slowly get back into range on the tail end of the Russian line. After a break of nearly two hours in the fighting, by 1735 hours Togo's division had approached to within 8km of the starboard quarter of the lagging *Poltava*, and *Mikasa* opened fire. Vice-Adm Dewa also returned with the *Yakumo* and Togo now concentrated the fire of all four of his battleships and three armored cruisers against the *Poltava*, hoping to finish off at least one Russian battleship. However, Capt Ivan P. Uspenskiy on the *Poltava* was not willing to go under without a fight and his gunners hit *Mikasa* several times. Even worse, the *Shimosa* shells proved to be incredibly unstable in battle and rounds burst inside gun barrels, disabling one 12-in gun on the *Shikishima* at 1745 hours and two 12-in guns on the *Asahi* at 1810 hours. *Mikasa*'s aft 12-in gun turret was hit twice at 1800 hours and another 12-in gun was temporarily out of action on the *Shikishima*, leaving Togo with only 11 of his 17 heavy guns still operational at the crucial moment of the action. Although the range had dropped to 8–9km, the Japanese 6-in and 8-in guns could not do much damage at this range. On the Russian side, the *Poltava* and *Peresvyet* were heavily damaged, but were still keeping formation.

*Retvizan*'s forward 12-in gun turret was hit by a Japanese *furoshiki* shell around 1815 hours; the shell exploded near the embrasure, setting fire to the canvas jacket on the gun barrels, and the over-pressure killed one man and wounded six others within the turret. The left gun was being loaded when the enemy shell hit and the concussion knocked the 741kg shell off its tray, crushing two more sailors. Fearing that fire would spread to the shell room below, the remaining crewmen flooded the area, which disabled all electrical circuits. Thus, *Retvizan* lost half its main armament, but the crew was able to bring the turret back into limited operation within one hour.

By 1830 hours the range had decreased to 7km but Togo was having difficulty controlling the distribution of fire of his battle line; *Shikishima* and *Asahi* were concentrating on the limping *Poltava* with their five 12-in guns, *Fuji* was firing at *Pobeda* and *Peresvyet*, and *Mikasa* was firing at *Tsesarevich* with its two 12-in guns. No Japanese ships were firing at the *Sevastopol* or *Retvizan*, allowing them to concentrate on the *Mikasa*. Moments later, *Mikasa* was hit by two more 12-in rounds and a 6-in round, causing 40 casualties. Sunset was now less than half an hour away and the Japanese pursuit seemed to be staggering under the impact of accurate Russian salvoes. Togo's flagship was almost no longer combat-effective but he signaled by semaphore to the *Asahi* to take over firing on the lead Russian ships, hoping for a miracle to stop the enemy's escape. At 1840 hours, Togo got his lucky break when *Asahi* fired a salvo at the *Tsesarevich* and scored two 12-in hits on the bridge.

Vice-Adm Vitgeft and two of his staff officers were blown to bits by the two 12-in hits, which also smashed in the roof of the conning tower and killed the steersman. Capt Nikolai M. Ivanov was badly wounded. The helm was jammed to port by the wreckage and the *Tsesarevich* suddenly swung off course, dutifully followed by the rest of the squadron. Within minutes, the *Tsesarevich* came to a virtual dead stop, throwing the

### Damage to battleships in Battle of Yellow Sea, August 10, 1904

| Name | Hits | Casualties |
|---|---|---|
| *Tsesarevich* | Hit by 13 12-in and 2 8-in shells | 12 killed, 47 wounded |
| *Pobieda* | 11 hits from large shells | 4 killed, 29 wounded |
| *Peresvyet* | 39 hits | 13 killed, 69 wounded |
| *Poltava* | 12–14 8–12-in hits | 12 killed, 43 wounded |
| *Retvizan* | 18 hits from 8–12-in shells | 6 killed, 42 wounded |
| *Sevastopol* | Hit by several shells | 1 killed, 62 wounded |
| *Mikasa* | Hit 20 times. Aft 12-in gun turret knocked out | 125 casualties |
| *Asahi* | 1 12-in hit near waterline<br>Both aft 12-in guns burst | 2 wounded |
| *Shikishima* | 1 forward 12-in gun burst | |

Russian squadron formation into total chaos. Rear Adm Prince Pavel Ukhtomski, the second-in-command in the *Peresvyet*, soon realized that the flagship was incapacitated and struggled to signal the other battleships to follow him, but his signal was not immediately noticed. The column of battleships fell into disorder as some ships went to port and others to starboard to avoid a pile-up behind the crippled *Tsesarevich*. Seeing the Russian flagship fall out, Togo ordered all his ships to concentrate fire upon the *Tsesarevich*.

While Prince Ukhtomski tried to gain command over the squadron, Capt Eduard Shchensnovich in the *Retvizan* boldly moved to draw fire off the damaged flagship by turning toward Togo's battle line. The *Retvizan*, despite being down by the bow with over 500 tons of water in several flooded compartments, sailed directly toward all four of Togo's battleships firing everything it had. Frantically, the Japanese battleships shifted fire to the *Retvizan* and hit it repeatedly; the range rapidly dropped to about 3.1km and the ship was pounded by every gun in Togo's battle line. Indeed, there were so many shell splashes around *Retvizan* that Japanese gunners had great difficulty determining their own fall of shot and their rangefinders were unable to compensate for the changes in distance. The editor of the Port Arthur newspaper *New Edge*, E. K. Nozhin, witnessed the *Retvizan*'s charge from the hospital ship *Mongolia*: "the *Retvizan*'s steel bulk appeared as a giant steaming boiler. Enormous columns of water rose continuously around it. The enemy directed the entire force of his gun fire toward the *Retvizan*, using shells of all calibers." However, Togo decided to play it safe; his battleships were running low on ammunition and too many of his 12-in guns were out of action, so he decided to hand the battle over to his light forces now that the Russian squadron was in disorder. Togo ordered his battleships to turn away – thus ending their role in the battle – and ordered his cruisers and destroyers to attack. Just as Togo was beginning to turn away, *Retvizan* was hit by several shells, one of which severely wounded Capt Shchensnovich in the stomach, and *Retvizan* also turned away, laying smoke. *Retvizan*'s dramatic charge had effectively ended the battleship duel.

During the entire day, *Retvizan* fired a total of 77 305mm shells (four AP, 73 common), 310 152mm shells (51 AP, 241 HE, 18 segmented), 341 75mm shells and 290 47mm shells. After the hit near the bridge, Midshipman V. Svin'inym took over the single Barr & Stroud FA2 rangefinder and controlled the battleship's fire as it retreated. The *Retvizan* had been hit a total of 21 times, including at least 18 large-caliber hits, but had no serious fires and both its armament and engine machinery were still intact. Japanese shellfire had only disabled one 6-in gun, two 75mm guns and five 47mm guns. Personnel losses were 6 killed and 43 wounded, or only 6 percent of the crew. Photos of the *Retvizan* taken after the battle indicate that many of the Japanese shells detonated prematurely, showering the battleship with fragments, but causing very little damage.

Although the situation looked grim for the Russian squadron, Togo failed to take advantage of the enemy's confusion. Prince Ukhtomski gradually got the *Pobeda*, *Sevastopol*, *Poltava* and the cruiser *Pallada* to follow him back to Port Arthur, while *Retvizan* proceeded on its own. After 20 minutes, the senior officer on the *Tsesarevich* was able to regain control of the ship and together with three destroyers they headed toward the British port of Kiaochou. The rest of the cruisers and destroyers split up; the *Askold* and one destroyer ran for Shanghai, the *Diana* went to Saigon and the *Novik* made for

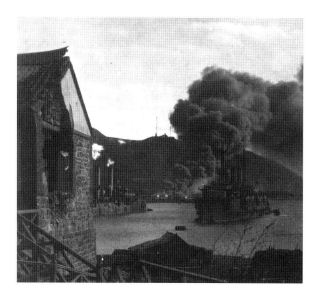

The *Pobieda* (right) is hit by 30 11-in howitzer shells on December 7 and settles into the harbor mud. Like most of the Russian squadron sunk at Port Arthur, she is later raised and incorporated into the Japanese Navy. (Library of Congress)

Vladivostok. Amazingly, Togo's numerically superior force was unable to stop the escape of a single Russian warship from the area of the battle. The Japanese destroyers had been kept too far back from the battle and by the time they swung into action, Ukhtomski had his five ships back in formation heading for Port Arthur. The secondary batteries and small-caliber guns on the Russians battleships fired repeatedly at the pursuing Japanese destroyers, forcing them to conduct their torpedo attacks from beyond 1.5km. Consequently, the Japanese destroyers fired 74 torpedoes, but achieved only a single hit on the cruiser *Pallada*. By 0700 hours on August 11, all five Russian battleships were back inside Port Arthur. Even the battered *Tsesarevich* made it to safety in Kiaochou, where it was interned by Japan's ally.

After the Battle of the Yellow Sea, the 1st Pacific Squadron remained sullenly in port, awaiting destruction. On December 5, 1904, Japanese ground troops finally captured 203-Meter Hill overlooking the harbor and observers immediately began to direct accurate fire onto the Russian battleships, only 5.7km away. In three days, the Japanese sank all the Russian battleships except for *Sevastopol,* which left the inner harbor. After a protracted battle against the numerous Japanese torpedo attacks which crippled his ship, Capt von Essen scuttled the *Sevastopol* on January 2, 1905. The 1st Pacific Squadron was gone.

# REINFORCEMENTS FROM THE BALTIC

It had been part of Russian naval strategy since 1897 that in the event of war with Japan, additional battleships would be sent from the Baltic to reinforce the squadron at Port Arthur. Indeed, Russian naval strategy for the Far East was based on avoiding a general fleet action until reinforcements arrived, ensuring a decisive numerical edge. Vice-Adm Zinovy P. Rozhestvensky, the Tsar's pet gunnery expert, was placed in command of the newly christened 2nd Pacific Squadron, which initially would consist of only the newest battleships and cruisers. However, as news from the Far East of one Russian defeat after another arrived in St Petersburg, the Naval Ministry kept adding more ships to the fleet, including the battleships *Sissoi Veliki* and *Navarin*. Eventually, even the older battleship *Imperator Nikolai I* and several other elderly warships were added.

Although much attention has focused on the alleged obsolescence of many of the Russian ships added to Rozhestvensky's squadron, the real problems with the 2nd Pacific Squadron were lack of training and the manner in which crews were thrown together. The core ships in the force – the four *Borodino*-class battleships *Borodino, Suvorov, Aleksandr III* and *Orel* – were still fitting out in the summer of 1904 and they were unable to conduct any serious gunnery training or squadron maneuvers before the fleet sailed. The *Oslyabya* had been in commission for over a year, but had spent most of that time in its abortive trip to the Red Sea, returning to the Baltic just in time to leave again. Consequently, the five main battleships in the 2nd Pacific Squadron lacked the experience and training of the crews in the 1st Pacific Squadron. Since most of the trained manpower was already in the Far East or with the Black Sea Fleet, the Naval Ministry decided to outfit the new battleships in the Baltic with the new conscripts from the class of 1904, as well as recalled reservists and engineers from the merchant marine. Thus, the crews on Rozhestvensky's battleships consisted of too many untrained conscripts and sullen reservists, mingled in with troublemakers and agitators from other ships in the Baltic Fleet. Oddly, the best-trained crews in Rozhestvensky's fleet were on the older battleships *Navarin* and *Sissoi Veliki*, many of whom had served in the Far East in 1901.

The battleship *Peresvyet* was destroyed in Port Arthur on December 7, 1904, after being struck by 23 11-in shells. The Russian battleships proved highly vulnerable to plunging fire and the roof of the stern 10-in gun turret has been blown off by an internal explosion. (Dmitri Malkov)

Rozhestvensky's 2nd Pacific Squadron was not able to depart Libau in Latvia until October 15, 1904, delayed by the difficulty in arranging for at-sea coaling. After a seven-month accident-filled voyage Rozhestvensky's fleet finally reached Cam Ranh Bay on May 9, where it was joined by additional warships in Rear Adm Nebogatov's 3rd Pacific Squadron. Although unhappy about the addition of these second-rate warships to his command, Rozhestvensky made the decision to proceed directly to Vladivostok through the Tsushima Straits.

Meanwhile, Togo spent the winter months shuttling his battle-weary battleships to Sasebo for repairs, including replacing their worn 12-in gun barrels. After the poor showing of the *furoshiki* shells, the decision was made to offload the remaining *Shimosa*-filled shells and substitute older common shells filled with standard black powder. The unreliable *Ijuin* fuse was also replaced with a less sensitive fuse, which was procured from Krupp. After the fall of Port Arthur, Togo moved his battleship division to the port of Masan in southern Korea, where he began intensive sub-caliber gunnery training. Meanwhile, a string of radio-equipped Japanese scout ships was deployed to detect the Russian 2nd Pacific Squadron – which Togo was following through international media reports – when it entered the waters around Japan.

# THE BATTLE OF TSUSHIMA MAY 27, 1905

*The fate of the Empire depends upon today's events. Let every man do his utmost.*

Togo's signal to fleet, morning of May 27, 1905

After traveling 29,000km, Rozhestvensky's fleet began to enter the Eastern Channel – a 50km-wide gap between the islands of Tsushima and Iki – in the pre-dawn darkness of May 27, 1905. The Russian formation was dispersed over a fairly large area and sailing in six separate columns, which made command and control very difficult in conditions of reduced visibility. Rozhestvensky led the 1st Division in the *Suvorov*, followed by *Aleksandr III*, *Borodino* and *Orel*. A group of two light cruisers and four destroyers covered his starboard side, facing the Japanese coast. Behind and to port, the *Oslyabya* led the 2nd Division,[11] followed by *Sissoi Veliki*, *Navarin* and the cruiser *Nakhimov*. Further back, Rear Adm Nebogatov led the 3rd Division in the battleship *Nicholas I*, followed by his three coast defense ships, and

---

11 Rear Admiral Felkerzam, commander of the 2nd Division, died of cancer two days prior to the battle but Rozhestvensky decided to keep this secret from the fleet. Captain Ber in the *Oslyabya* was nominally in charge of the 2nd Division. Rear Admiral Nebogatov was unaware that he was de facto second-in-command.

## ENGAGING THE ENEMY

A view of the battleship *Mikasa* as seen through the Liuzhol rangefinder on board *Poltava*.

A view of the battleship *Suvorov* shortly after being hit, as seen through the Barr & Stroud rangefinder aboard *Mikasa*.

a cruiser division shepherding the auxiliaries. In the very rear of the formation were two hospital ships.

On the eve of battle, the bulk of the Japanese naval strength was waiting on the Korean coast in Masan: Togo's 1st Division (four battleships, two armored cruisers), Vice-Adm Kamimura's 2nd Division (six armored cruisers) and Rear Adm Uryu's 4th Division (four protected cruisers). Japanese intelligence had lost track of Rozhestvensky's fleet and Togo was uncertain if the Russians would come through the Tsushima Strait in a direct course for Vladivostok or circle round Japan and go for the La Perouse Strait in the north. Togo had to prepare for both possibilities, so he loaded up as much coal as possible on his battleships and waited for the Russian fleet to be spotted. The only Japanese ships actually guarding the Tsushima Straits were Rear Adm Togo's four cruisers in the 6th Division in the Eastern Channel, Vice-Adm Kataoka's 5th Division with the captured Chinese battleship *Chinyen* and three protected cruisers in the Western Channel, supplemented by a few armed merchant cruisers. Vice-Adm Dewa's 3rd Division and five destroyer flotillas waited in Miura Bay on Tsushima Island. At this time, the weather was poor in the Tsushima Strait and visibility was limited, making it possible for the blacked-out Russian warships to slip through the strait undetected. However, the Russian hospital ship *Orel* in the rear of the formation kept its lights on and was spotted at 0330 hours by a Japanese armed merchant cruiser, which promptly radioed Togo.

As soon as he was alerted to the Russian activity in the Eastern Channel, Togo ordered his ships to dump their extra coal and begin preparing for battle. At 0505 hours, Togo steamed out of Masan with all three divisions, while *Mikasa's* band played

## ENGAGING THE ENEMY

Most of the Russian battleships relied upon the **Liuzhol rangefinder** introduced in the 1880s, which was effective out to 4,000 yards. The Liuzhol rangefinder measured the distance between two known vertical points on the target, in this case from the forward lookout nest to the waterline. The *Poltava's* gunnery officer in the conning tower then took the data obtained and consulted reference books and charts, which enabled him to calculate the range to the target, as well as the elevation and deflection required to hit it. He would then transmit this data to the gun crews by means of an electro-mechanical indicator system known as the Geisler M1893/94. Once the battleship fired at the target, the gunnery officer had to spot the shell splashes and estimate the necessary corrections, sending this along via the Geisler system as well. In a large fleet action, multiple shell splashes from several ships firing 12-inch and 6-inch shells made it very difficult for the gunnery officer to correct his own ship's fire.

The Japanese battleships relied upon the Barr & Stroud FA3 coincidence rangefinders, which had only been introduced in 1903. The system used two telescopes mounted on a tube and the gunnery officer looked through the single eyepiece located in the center of the rangefinder. Although the gunnery officer initially saw two reticule images, by turning a dial he could superimpose both images horizontally until they overlaid each other in a single image. When the gunnery officer achieved this single image, he could then read the distance to target off a scale. The coincidence rangefinders were accurate to about 6,000 yards and much quicker to use than the time-consuming Liuzhol rangefinder.

Vice-Admiral Rozhestvensky – a screaming imbecile of a commander, promoted well past his abilities. Even before Tsushima, Rozhestvensky was suffering from a near mental breakdown, and once in the presence of the enemy he was unable to assemble his fleet into a proper battle line. (Author's collection)

the naval anthem on her aft deck. Togo headed east at 14 knots, hoping to intercept Rozhestvensky to the north-east of Tsushima. Since the distance from Masan to the battle area was about 160km, it would take six hours of steaming to intercept the Russian fleet. In the meantime, Japanese scouting forces moved in to pinpoint the Russian position and by 0700 hours they were shadowing Rozhestvensky's fleet. Japanese cruisers sent regular radio reports on the enemy to Togo, as he drew nearer to the Tsushima Strait. As the number of Japanese vessels steaming parallel to the Russian fleet increased, individual ship captains – who had been given no specific pre-battle orders by Rozhestvensky – became increasingly jittery in the presence of the enemy. On his own initiative, Capt Nikolai V. Jung of the *Orel* opened fire on one of the Japanese cruisers at a range of 9km, in an effort to drive it off. Several other ships joined in – indicating the lack of fire control in Rozhestvensky's fleet – and *Orel* fired about 30 rounds before the command to cease fire was obeyed. Dewa's cruisers backed off a bit but remained within visual range and continued to report Russian movements to Togo.

As noon approached and the Japanese cruisers continued to hover on his flanks, Rozhestvensky became convinced that a fleet action was imminent. He was certain that the Japanese cruisers on his port side – now ten ships – would mount an attack and he decided to try and form the 1st and 2nd Divisions into a single battle line, but signaling confusion and poorly trained bridge crews resulted in a chaotic muddle. Instead of one battle line, Rozhestvensky ended up with the 1st Division to the right of the main column, now consisting of the 2nd and 3rd Divisions. Efforts to reorganize the fleet only added to the confusion and Rozhestvensky's fleet was still trying to get into a single column when Togo's main fleet was spotted at 1319 hours, about 11.2km to the north-east. Togo's fleet was in a single column, led by the *Mikasa* and the rest of the 1st Division, followed by Kamimura's 2nd Division.

Japanese radio reporting was not entirely accurate and Togo had been misinformed about the correct location of the Russian fleet, so he ended up appearing on Rozhestvensky's starboard bow, closest to the newest Russian battleships. Togo wanted to avoid a head-on clash with the four *Borodino*-class battleships until the Russian fleet had been pounded for a while, so he boldly decided to cut across the front of the advancing Russian fleet and conduct a sharp U-turn to bring his fleet on a parallel course on Rozhestvensky's port quarter. The Russians were astounded as the Japanese fleet charged across their front without firing and then began to execute a high-speed turn at 1355 hours, each ship pivoting at the same spot. Only a very confident commander would have executed such a bold move so close to the enemy since the Russian rangefinders would quickly get a good firing solution on the fixed turning point and the Japanese ships would be partly masked for at least 10–15 minutes.

Rozhestvensky hesitated for nearly ten minutes, watching the Japanese battle line begin its turn, until he finally ordered his battleships to commence fire. The *Suvorov* opened fire at the *Mikasa* at 1405 hours at a range of 5.8km and was soon joined by the rest of the 1st Division. Capt 2nd Rank Vladimir Semenoff, on the *Suvorov*, watched through his Zeiss binoculars:

> The shots which went over and those which fell short were all close, but the most interesting, i.e. the hits, as in the fight of 10th August, could not be seen. Our shells on bursting emitted scarcely any smoke, and the fuses were adjusted to burst inside after penetrating the target. A hit could only be detected when something fell – and nothing fell! In a couple of minutes, when the *Fuji* and *Asahi* had turned also and were following the first ships, the enemy began to reply.

In fact, the *Mikasa* was nearly hit with the first salvo, which fell only 20m astern, and she was hit 15 times in the next five minutes. Russian accuracy was fairly good, and the *Borodino*-class battleships were firing broadsides of about four 12-in rounds and 18 6-in rounds every minute. By 1409 hours the Japanese battle line had completed its turn and was now roughly parallel to the front part of the Russian fleet. Togo ordered an increase to 15 knots and all four battleships and eight armored cruisers opened fire. Japanese battleships opened the action firing common shells, intended to start fires. Semenoff noted:

> The first shells flew over us. At this range some of the long ones turned a complete somersault, and could clearly be seen with the naked eye curving like so many sticks thrown in the air. They flew over us, making a sort of wail, different to the ordinary roar… After them came others short of us – nearer and nearer. Splinters whistled through the air, jingled against the side and superstructure. Then, quite close and abreast the foremost funnel, rose a gigantic pillar of smoke, water and flame. The next shell struck the side by the center 6-in turret, and there was a tremendous noise behind and below me on the port quarter. Smoke and tongues of fire leapt out of the officers' gangway; a shell having fallen into the captain's cabin, and having penetrated the deck, had burst in the officers' quarters, setting them on fire.

The main gunnery duel pitted 12 Japanese ships against 14 Russian ships, eight of which were battleships. The Russians had an edge in terms of heavy guns, with 26 12-in and 16 10-in guns versus only 16 12-in and one 10-in gun on Togo's ships. However, the Japanese heavy guns had twice the rate of fire of their Russian counterparts and their fire control was excellent. By running parallel for over 40 minutes and at less than 6km, the Japanese could use their Barr & Stroud FA3 rangefinders to accurately put their rounds on target. The Japanese also had a decisive

The sunken battleship *Retvizan*. It was hit by 13 11-in howitzer shells on December 6, 1904, which caused extensive damage. The skeleton crew left aboard scuttled the hulk to prevent its quick re-use by the Japanese. (Naval Historical Center, NH94780)

# BATTLE OF TSUSHIMA
## MAY 27, 1905, 1515 HOURS

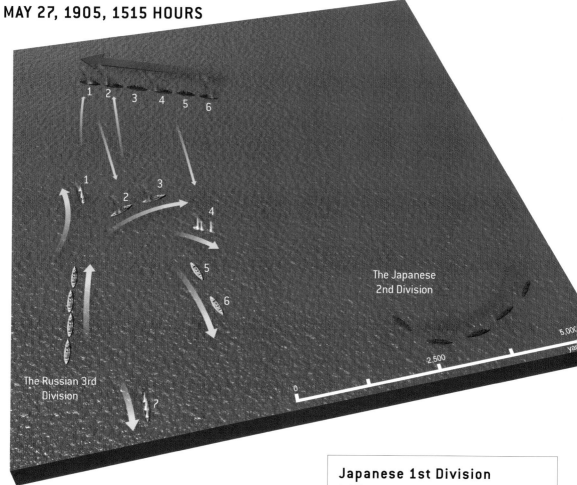

The Japanese
2nd Division

5,000

2,500

yar

0

The Russian 3rd
Division

## Key
General direction of Japanese Fleet Divisions
Evasive tactics of Russian Fleet
Lines of fire
Direct hit on a ship
Burning ship

## Japanese 1st Division
1. *Mikasa*
2. *Shikishima*
3. *Fuji*
4. *Asahi*
5. *Kashin*
6. *Nisshin*

## Russian Fleet
1. *Suvorov*
2. *Orel*
3. *Borodino*
4. *Aleksandr III*
5. *Navarin*
6. *Sissoi Veliki*
7. *Oslyabya*

The Russian fleet begins to fall apart at 1515 hours as Rozhestvensky is wounded
and both *Suvorov* and *Oslyabya* fall out of line. Unlike the Japanese, who can still
concentrate fire from their 1st Division battleships on the *Orel* and *Borodino*, the
Russian fleet is collapsing into uncoordinated, leaderless efforts which dissipate
their remaining firepower.

two-to-one advantage in medium-caliber guns, with 30 8-in and 80 6-in guns that could be brought to bear, versus only four 9-in, eight 8-in and 45 6-in guns on the Russian side. Unlike the Battle of the Yellow Sea, Tsushima was fought at ranges that allowed the medium-caliber weapons to play a major role.

The Russian battleships in the lead concentrated most of their fire on the *Mikasa* and *Shikishima*, and although they were able to achieve numerous hits, none were critical. In the rear of the Russian formation, the older battleships concentrated on Kamimura's tail-end cruisers. Togo split the fire of his force, with *Mikasa* and *Asahi* engaging the *Suvorov*, while *Shikishima*, *Fuji*, *Nisshin* and *Kasuga* engaged the closer *Oslyabya*. Although the Russian battle line had a greater number of heavy guns, the Japanese fire quickly began to gain the upper hand for two reasons. First, the Japanese quick-firing guns were together firing over 300rpm at the two lead Russian ships, which led to a large number of hits. Second, the Japanese were using high explosive shells that succeeded in inflicting significant damage on the upper works of their targets, while the Russians were firing mostly armor-piercing rounds at their enemy's hulls, with many rounds landing short of the target. Semenoff noted the change in Japanese gunnery tactics, writing that in comparison with the Battle of the Yellow Sea:

> Shells seemed to be pouring upon us incessantly, one after another. It seemed as if these were mines, not shells, which were striking the ship's side and falling on the deck. They burst as soon as they touched anything – the moment they encountered the least impediment in their flight. Handrails, funnel guys, topping lifts of the boats' derricks, were quite sufficient to cause a thoroughly efficient burst. The steel plates and superstructure on the upper deck were torn to pieces, and the splinters caused many casualties. Iron ladders were crumpled up into rings, and guns were literally hurled from their mountings. Such havoc would never be caused by the simple impact of a shell, still less by that of its splinters. It could only be caused by the force of the explosion. In addition to this, there was the unusual high temperature and liquid flame of the explosion, which seemed to spread over everything.

The *Oslyabya* was the first to feel the torrent of Japanese fire. Two sailors named Kora and Suslenko, who had been convicted of serious offenses, were ordered to stand on the deck next to the forward 10-in gun turret as the ship went into action. The men were told that if they left this position they would be shot by the ship's senior officer. In any case, *Oslyabya's* forward 10-in turret fired only three salvoes before it was hit in quick succession by two large-caliber rounds, which knocked it out. Koral and Suslenko were blown to pieces. Japanese 6-in gunfire hit the forward bridge and mainmast, knocking out the Barr & Stroud rangefinder, and mortally

Admiral Togo on the bridge of the *Mikasa* at the start of the Battle of Tsushima. Note the Japanese officer using the FA3 rangefinder behind Togo. The ship's compass has hammocks wrapped around it for protection from splinters. Chief Gunnery Officer Lieutenant Commander Abo Kiyokazu is behind the compass, looking at Togo. (Naval Historical Center)

wounding the gunnery officer. Shell fragments also severed the electrical cables for the Geisler fire-control system, reducing all the remaining guns to local control, for which they were not trained. Within 20 minutes of the gunnery duel beginning, three of the six portside 6-in guns on *Oslyabya* were knocked out and her remaining guns were firing only occasionally and ineffectively.

> Another shell exploded in front of the conning tower. Of the drummer who had been on duty there, nothing was left but a headless and legless trunk. Shell-splinters flew through the loopholes into the interior of the tower. Steersman Prokyus, who was at the wheel, was killed outright. The staff officers and the ship's officers were wounded.[12]

With the bridge crew momentarily disabled, the *Oslyabya* swung out of line at 1425 hours and Kamimura's six cruisers now raked her upper works viciously with 6-in and 76mm gunfire. As the distance between the fleets fell below 5km around 1420 hours, the Japanese battleships switched to using armor-piercing rounds. One of these 12-in AP shells struck the *Oslyabya* on the port side just aft of the 10-in gun turret, punching through the thin armor plate and causing serious flooding. Shortly thereafter, another 12-in round struck near the port hawser hole, throwing the anchor into the sea and tearing a gaping hole in the unarmored bow. Despite her damage, *Oslyabya* was still moving at about 10 knots and the forward motion forced more and more water into the hull, causing a rapid list to port. Flooding soon shut down the two forward dynamos, which led to loss of power to both pumps and to ammunition hoists. In a foolish attempt to counterbalance the list to port, the *Oslyabya*'s senior officer ordered the starboard magazine flooded but this only caused the bow to dip further under the water. The counter-flooding destroyed *Oslyabya*'s remaining stability and the ship rapidly heeled over to port until its funnels were touching the water. In his last moments, Capt Vladimir Ber ordered the crew to abandon ship and surprisingly, over 40 percent of the crew made it into the water before *Oslyabya* capsized at 1315 hours. The overturned wreck remained afloat for a while, but then finally sank with her starboard screw still turning, taking Capt Ber and 470 of her crew with her. This was the first modern battleship sunk entirely by gunfire and the Russian crews on the remaining ships that passed her grave site were astonished at how quickly it had happened.

The battleship *Asahi* suffered nine hits at Tsushima, causing eight killed and 23 wounded, but her performance was not significantly affected. Battleships built with the British casemate style of protection could absorb a large amount of damage from standard armor-piercing shot. (Naval Historical Center, NH58981)

12 Novoy-Pribikov, *Tsushima*.

While *Oslyabya* was being pounded into a flaming wreck, the Russians were able to inflict some damage on Togo's battle line. *Mikasa*, *Asahi* and *Shikishima* were all hit, although none seriously. The flagship *Suvorov* was also receiving a severe pounding at this time and both of her 12-in turrets were soon out of action. Japanese 6-in shells repeatedly hit the fore bridge and the conning tower, showering the area with fragments that rapidly killed or wounded most of the bridge crew, including Rozhestvensky. Hit in the head by a fragment, "Rozhestvensky stooped lower and lower to avoid the hail of splinters,"[13] which only served to reduce his situational awareness about the ongoing battle. Aboard the Russian battleships, the fires spread rapidly due to a failure to adequately remove combustible items before battle and the inability of untrained crews to fight fires while under bombardment. Semenoff noted:

> The stupor which seems to come over men, who have never been in action before, when the first shells begin to fall … The men at the fire mains and hoses stood as if mesmerized, gazing at the smoke and flames, not understanding, apparently, what was happening. I went down to them from the bridge, and with the most commonplace words, such as "Wake up! Turn the water on!" got them to pull themselves together and bravely to fight the fire.

However, Japanese shellfire soon destroyed many of the hoses and wounded the crew members on *Suvorov*'s open deck, severely reducing its damage-control capabilities. Despite the horrendous damage and casualties, the *Suvorov*'s crew fought bravely at their stations until killed or wounded. Semenoff saw Lt P. E. Vladimirskiy, the senior gunnery officer, manning the rangefinder. "[He] shouted his orders in a clear voice, and the electricians quickly turned the handles of the indicator, transmitting the range to the turrets and light gun batteries." Vladimirskiy was soon wounded and a Japanese shell destroyed the rangefinder and its crew. At around 1443 hours a Japanese salvo disabled the *Suvorov*'s steering gear and it turned sharply to starboard, almost colliding with the ships following.

By 1445 hours, the Russian fleet formation was beginning to fall apart under the barrage of Japanese high explosives. Aside from the cruiser *Asama*, Togo still had 11 ships operational in his battle line, although both *Mikasa* and *Nisshin* had received considerable damage. *Aleksandr III*, *Borodino* and *Orel* all had serious fires on board, mostly concentrated in their central sections on the spar decks. Around 1500 hours, the Japanese scored another hit on *Suvorov*'s conning tower and this time, Rozhestvensky was felled with a splinter in his skull. The same shell wounded Capt Vasiliy V. Ignatsius and killed both helmsmen, which resulted in *Suvorov* swinging sharply to starboard, steaming out of control in a circle. Capt Nikolai M. Bukhvostov in the *Aleksandr III* took the lead and changed the heading of the formation to due north in an effort to cut behind the rear of Togo's line. However, Togo deftly ordered each of his ships to execute a turn and quickly brought his battle line back to the west to rake the *Aleksandr III* and *Orel*. The Russian cruiser *Zhemchug* responded with a torpedo attack to drive off Togo's battleships,

OVERLEAF
At 1410 hours on May 27 1905, the Japanese battleline, led by the battleship *Mikasa*, then the *Shikishima*, *Fuji* and *Asahi* began concentrating on the *Oslyabya* at a range of 6,800 meters. Initially, the Japanese battleships fired high explosive rounds, which set numerous fires on the upperworks of the *Oslyabya*. Togo's battleships fired at twice the rate of the Russian battleships and quickly gained firepower superiority. As the range dropped, Togo switched to armor-piercing rounds, one of which pierced the thin armor plate on the *Oslyabya*'s bow. Japanese cruisers also joined in the bombardment, pummeling the doomed *Oslyabya* with a fusillade of 6-in and 8-in gunfire. Although *Mikasa* had already been hit more than fifteen times by this point, she displayed no visible signs of damage.

---

13 Novoy-Pribikov, *Tsushima*.

The battleship *Orel* in the Baltic in 1904. At Tsushima, *Orel* suffered 30 killed and 100 wounded and was the only one of the four *Borodino*-class battleships to survive the battle. (Naval Historical Center, NH45853)

The Japanese armored cruiser *Nisshin*. In order to redress his inferiority in battleships at both Yellow Sea and Tsushima, Togo was forced to use armored cruisers in his battle line. (Naval Historical Center, NH58668)

but was itself driven off in a hail of 6- and 8-in gunfire. Seeing the *Suvorov* limping away to the south-east, Togo ordered the Japanese battle line to increase fire on the crippled Russian flagship – he did not want it to escape like *Tsesarevich* had at Yellow Sea. Forgetting about the rest of the Russian fleet for a moment, Togo ordered some of his ships to close within 2.7km of the crippled *Suvorov* and finish her off.

Bukhvostov tried to take the heat off *Suvorov* by repeating Shchensnovich's move at Yellow Sea – around 1600 hours he turned *Aleksandr III* directly toward Togo's fleet in an effort to push them back. Shortly thereafter, the *Borodino*, now in the lead, turned the fleet due south and disappeared into the mist. Unlike the *Retvizan's* charge, the Japanese were able to shift fires upon the rapidly approaching *Aleksandr III*, whose forward section and bridge were hit by several salvoes. Although *Aleksandr III* was badly damaged, it had enabled the Russian fleet to escape the ferocious Japanese bombardment. Even the crippled *Suvorov* was able to steam south at 9 knots, until Togo's battleships lost sight of her.

Interestingly, Rear Adm Nebogatov's much-maligned 3rd Division in the rear, being less of a target for Togo's battle line, was able to focus its fire on some of Kamimura's armored cruisers, such as *Yagumo*. The *Nisshin* was hit by three 12-in and one 9-in round from the *Nikolai I* between 1500 and 1600 hours, including one which wounded Vice-Adm Misu, Togo's second-in-command. The Russians used the respite to put out some of the fires on *Suvorov* and *Aleksandr III*, but Rear Adm Nebogatov was still located near the rear of the column in *Nikolai I* and unaware that Rozhestvensky's injury now placed him in command. Amazingly, the crippled *Suvorov* caught up with the tail end of the column but its steering was too badly damaged to stay with the formation. During this lull, a Russian destroyer came alongside the still-burning *Suvorov* and took aboard the wounded Rozhestvensky, Vladimir Semenoff and two other officers. Midshipman Werner von Kursel, the only remaining uninjured officer aboard the *Suvorov*, volunteered to remain and thus a midshipman was left in charge of the fleet's flagship. Meanwhile, after heading south for over 30 minutes and avoiding serious contact, Kamimura's cruisers appeared on the port quarter of the Russian squadron. Togo had sent his cruisers ahead at high speed to regain contact and they immediately radioed the Russians' heading.

Capt Petr I. Serebrennikov in the lead *Borodino* was now the de facto fleet commander, with Rozhestvensky unconscious and Nebogatov tamely following in the rear. Sighting Kamimura's closing cruisers at about 1705 hours, Serebrennikov decided to turn hard to starboard and resume heading to the north. Although Togo's battleships were over

14km to the north-east, the 4-knot speed advantage was now used to rapidly close the gap and by the time that the Russian squadron had completed its turn 15 minutes later, the *Mikasa* was only 6.5km away. Togo rapidly executed his own turn to starboard, bringing his battleships on a northerly heading, nearly parallel to the Russian squadron.

The Russian battleships were in poor shape for another gunnery duel. *Borodino* had a heavy list to starboard from a hit near the waterline, but her aft 12-in gun turret was still operational. *Aleksandr III* was probably in the best condition, with her fires under control, but her crew had suffered significant casualties. The *Orel* had suffered severe fire and blast damage to her upper works and her demoralized crew was on the verge of panic. The ships of the 2nd and 3rd Divisions were still reasonably intact, but merely tagging along behind the battered 1st Division. At this point, the Russian fleet had no functional senior leadership or direction, resulting in a "herd mentality" once ships began to fall out from damage.

After a two-hour break, the battle resumed in earnest around 1800 hours as Togo closed to within 6.3km of the Russian starboard rear quarter. *Borodino* was in the lead, followed by *Orel, Sissoi Veliki, Aleksandr III, Navarin*, and the *Nikolai I*. This time, the Russians had lost their advantage in heavy guns, since they had only a few operational 12-in gun turrets left, while Togo's firepower was almost the same. The Japanese battleships concentrated their fire on the *Borodino* and *Aleksandr III*, which could only return weak fire. Both Russian battleships were soon listing heavily to starboard from numerous hits, which made it difficult to use their remaining armament. At 1830 hours, another Japanese salvo hit the *Aleksandr III*, which veered sharply to port and heeled over. The capsized *Aleksandr III* remained afloat for a half hour then sank at 1907 hours. There were no survivors from her 825-man crew.

As the light began to wane, Togo sensed that the gunnery duel was nearly over and that it was time to pursue the crippled Russian fleet. Although *Nisshin* was hit by another 12-in shell at 1900 hours, it was clear that Russian defensive firepower was nearly gone. The four torpedo boats of the 11th Torpedo Boat Division closed in on the burning *Suvorov*, now 15km south of the escaping Russian fleet. Midshipman von Kursel, manning a 75mm gun near her stern, desperately tried to drive these attackers off but the *Suvorov* was hit by one or more torpedoes and it rapidly capsized "in a thick cloud of dark yellow smoke." There were only 20 survivors from *Suvorov*'s crew.

*Borodino* managed to fend off the torpedo boats with her 75mm and 47mm guns, but she was burning furiously. At 1928 hours, Togo signaled his battleships to break off the action. Capt Matsumoto Kazu, commander of the *Fuji*, decided to fire the salvo that was already loaded before turning away. One of *Fuji*'s 12-in rounds struck *Borodino* below the starboard forward 6-in gun and set off the ready ammunition that caused a huge fire. With few men left to fight the flames, it spread to the

The Russian battleship *Imperator Nikolai I* suffered only five hits at Tsushima, including one 12-in hit. Although relatively intact, this battleship surrendered on May 28, 1905. (Naval Historical Center, NH92405)

nearby 6-in gun magazine which detonated at 1930 hours. Sympathetic detonations from adjacent magazines blew out her hull and *Borodino* quickly capsized and sank. The only survivor was Seaman 1st Class Semyon Yuschin, who was rescued after spending 12 hours in the sea.

*Orel* took the lead after *Borodino* sank and continued on a north-east course for Vladivostok. Finally realizing that he was in command, Rear Adm Nebogatov soon came up and took the lead with the *Nikolai I*, signaling, "Follow the admiral." The *Sissoi Veliki* and *Navarin* had both suffered significant hull damage in the second gunnery duel and were falling behind, so the formation slowed to about 9 knots. The continuing misty weather favored a Russian escape, but once again poor discipline gave away the Russian position. Around 2015 hours the *Navarin* switched on its searchlights to detect Japanese torpedo boats, but it only served to alert the Japanese to their location. Togo committed over 30 destroyers and torpedo boats to pursue Nebogatov's tattered command and they approached to within 300m in the darkness to launch their attacks. The *Navarin*, suffering flooding in her damaged stern, stopped to make repairs and was soon found by several Japanese destroyer flotillas. The *Navarin* managed to drive the diminutive craft off for a while, but around 2300 hours one finally got in close enough to torpedo her stern. Minutes later, another torpedo exploded amidships. Although the *Navarin* was crippled, her crew managed to keep her afloat for several more hours until the Japanese decided to pump two final torpedoes into her at 0215 hours on May 28. *Navarin* capsized and only three members of her 690-man crew were rescued.

Nebogatov's command continued to shrink during the night. *Sissoi Veliki*, unable to keep up with the formation, was left behind to fend for herself. In short order, Japanese destroyers attacked and blew off her rudder with a torpedo at 2315 hours. Capt Mikhail V. Oserov tried to steer toward Tsushima in the hope of beaching and saving his crew, but when Japanese warships approached her the next morning he decided to scuttle his ship. *Admiral Ushakov*, one of the coast defense battleships, was also left behind but she passed the night undetected by Japanese torpedo boats. The cruisers *Oleg*, *Aurora* and *Zhemchug* abandoned the effort to get to Vladivostok and headed south toward the Philippines. The other cruisers, destroyers and auxiliaries were either sunk or scattered. Nebogatov was left only with the *Orel*, the *Nikolai I*, the coastal defense battleships *Senyavin* and *Apraksin*, and the protected cruiser *Izumrud*. During the night, *Orel* was able to repair one of its 12-in gun turrets and two 6-in gun turrets.

By the morning of May 28, it looked as if Nebogatov's command had a chance to make it to Vladivostok after all. The ships had traveled about 320km from the scene of the battle during the night and their destination was now less than 500km away. However, the previous day's overcast weather gave way to a bright, sunny morning and by 0600 hours Vice-Adm Kataoka's cruisers had found Nebogatov's force and quickly reported their position. Togo spent the night resupplying his battleships and by 1000 hours he brought his battleships and armored cruisers out to encircle Nebogatov's slow-moving force near the Liancourt Rocks. Unwilling to risk losses now that the battle was won, Togo opted to fight a long-range gunnery duel rather than close as he had the day before.

The *Mikasa* shortly after the Battle of Tsushima. Note that the only damage evident is the loss of her rear topmast, but that her funnels are intact. (Naval Historical Center, NH101751)

The armored cruiser *Kasuga* opened fire first from 9.1km, and hit the *Nikolai I*'s funnel with its third salvo. Nebogatov's ships could not effectively engage Togo's battleships at that distance and they lacked the speed to close the distance, so at 1030 hours Nebogatov elected to surrender. Although the cruiser *Izumrud* refused to surrender and sped off, the Japanese captured the battered *Orel* and the *Nikolai I*, *Senyavin* and *Apraksin*.

However, it was fitting that the last operational Russian battleship in the Pacific should go down fighting rather than meekly surrendering. Capt V. N. Miklukha-Maklai in the coast defense battleship *Ushakov* was slowly chugging along in Nebogatov's wake when the armored cruisers *Iwate* and *Yakumo* discovered him around 1500 hours. Maklai had four 10-in/45-cal guns with better range than the eight 8-in guns and 26 6-in guns on the Japanese cruisers, but their low rate of fire was no match for the quick-firing Japanese guns. After only 30 minutes of dueling, the *Ushakov* was a burning wreck and casualties were heavy, so Maklai ordered the ship scuttled. The *Ushakov* capsized and sank with Maklai, but 328 of her crew were rescued. Japan's Combined Fleet had won the duel for supremacy in the Far East and Russian naval power in the Pacific had been decisively defeated.

Only 3½ months after Tsushima, on September 11, 1905, the battleship *Mikasa* was anchored at Sasebo when it suffered a massive magazine explosion that killed 339 crew members. The *Mikasa* sank in the shallow harbor and investigations revealed that decomposing nitrocellulose propellant was responsible for the disaster. Japan was fortunate that the *Mikasa* was not destroyed by its defective ammunition until after the war, since had Togo been lost on his flagship as Makarov had, the effect on Japanese morale would have been catastrophic.

A Japanese sailor stands guard on the *Orel* near the forward 12-in gun turret after its surrender at Tsushima. Note the damage to the port 12-in gun barrel and the lack of apparent damage to the bridge area. (Naval Historical Center, NH66269)

# STATISTICS AND ANALYSIS

In theory, IJN battleships had an advantage in firepower provided by higher rates of fire and better accuracy, but this did not always pan out on the battlefield. In summary, a Russian battleship could deliver a broadside of eight 12-in and about 35 6-in shells in a two-minute period, while in the same period, a Japanese battleship could deliver 12 12-in and 70 6-in shells. In a typical engagement at 7km in clear weather between fleets cruising parallel to each other, this would equate to about two to three hits for each Russian battleship firing and four to five hits for each Japanese battleship firing. Thus, the rate of hits would gradually influence a gunnery duel in Japan's favor, even though its guns lacked the ability at this range to penetrate Russian armor.

A close-up of the damage to the port forward 12-in gun barrel on the *Orel*. A hit from a large-caliber round shattered the end of the gun barrel, disabling this gun. (Naval Historical Center, NH66268)

The initial surface action on February 9, 1904 involved five Russian battleships and six cruisers engaging six Japanese battleships and six cruisers for 20 minutes at ranges of about 8km. Neither side had practiced gunnery against moving targets at such ranges before the war and each scored only 0.4–0.5 percent hits. Neither side suffered any significant damage in this first gunnery duel or demonstrated any innate technical superiority over the other.

The Battle of the Yellow Sea on August 10, 1904 was the most balanced fleet action of the war, with six Russian battleships and three cruisers versus four Japanese battleships and three cruisers. This battle was particularly unusual in that firing began at the unheard-of range of 13km and most of the gunnery duel took place between 6km and 8.5km. Despite the fact that neither side's rangefinders or training prepared them for this type of long-range gunnery, the accuracy was better than pre-war exercises would have suggested. Yellow Sea was primarily a contest between Togo's 12-in and 8-in guns versus Vitgeft's 12-in and 10-in guns, with medium-caliber 6-in guns playing only a minor role for most of the 232 minutes of combat. The Japanese battleships fired a total of 603 12-in rounds, of which 279 were armor piercing – none of which achieved any penetrations – and 324 were high explosive. Furthermore, the *Shimosa*-filled *furoshiki* shells proved to be a huge failure, since they proved very unstable and resulted in three burst 12-in gun barrels – reducing Togo's long-range firepower by nearly 25 percent. Overall, the Japanese scored about 30 hits with heavy guns, or 4.7 percent hits. The Russian battleships fired 483 10- and 12-in rounds (of which only about 5 percent were armor-piercing) and they achieved about 20 hits, or 4.1 percent hits. Although the Japanese battleships had a 24 percent higher rate of fire, they also expended their ammunition supply at a much higher rate and this influenced Togo to restrain ammunition expenditure later at the Battle of Tsushima. The Japanese battleships achieved more hits but this didn't lead to any great advantage since their AP shells were incapable of penetrating main belt armor at that range and many of the *Shimosa*-filled shells prematurely detonated. Nor were "dud rates" a major factor at Yellow Sea, since only two of 16 Russian 12-in rounds that hit failed to explode.

## Ammunition fired at the Battle of the Yellow Sea

| Ammunition | Japanese rounds fired | Russian rounds fired |
|---|---|---|
| 12-in | 603 | 259 |
| 10-in | 33 | 224 |
| 8-in | 307 | 0 |
| 6-in | 3,592 | 2,364 |

If anything, this battle indicated how difficult it was to sink a battleship using only slow-firing, long-range gunnery. Although both the *Mikasa* and five of six Russian battleships received at least six or more large-caliber hits, none were near sinking and fires were kept under control. The *Poltava*, which the Japanese had tried so hard to pulverize, had only two serious hits, one of which was a huge hole torn in its deck behind the forward 12-in turret – a hole characteristic of Lyddite or *Shimosa*. The *Peresvyet* suffered two 12-in hits on its starboard bow near the waterline, similar to the damage inflicted on *Oslyabya* at Tsushima, but *Peresvyet* did not sink. Even the battered *Tsesarevich* managed to escape. No Russian battleships suffered serious fire damage at Yellow Sea, which explains why no battleships were lost. Japanese performance at Yellow Sea was hindered by poor command and control, with Togo having great difficulty in getting his cruisers and torpedo boats into the action. Unlike at Tsushima, the Russian 1st Pacific Squadron maintained an effective single line of battle and its crews were adequately trained to keep in the fight.

Tsushima was less a battle than an execution of an untrained mob. Despite the fact that the overloaded *Borodino*-class battleships had most of their main armor belt submerged, Japanese gunnery was still unable to penetrate even the thinner upper-belt armor of the Russian battleships. After the disappointing performance at Yellow Sea, the *Shimosa*-filled shells were replaced by black powder-filled common shells and Togo resolved to get his powerful armored cruisers into the fight to support his outnumbered battleships. Togo also opted to get in closer than at Yellow Sea and the gunnery duels at Tsushima were conducted at 6km or less. Out of 11,096 medium- and large-caliber shells fired by Togo's warships, only 446 were 12-in rounds, which scored about 9 percent hits. By halving the range, Togo doubled his hit rate over Yellow Sea. However, much of the damage done at Tsushima was done by the barrage of 1,200 8-in and 9,450 6-in rounds fired by the Japanese ships, which smothered the Russian battleships in a "hail of fire." From post-battle examination, we know that the *Orel* suffered 55 hits, of which five were 12-in, two 10-in, nine 8-in and 39 6-in. At Yellow Sea, the Japanese scored five to six large-caliber hits on most of the Russian battleships but sank none of them – the crucial distinguishing feature was the large number of medium-caliber hits. The virtually untrained Russian battleship crews could not compete with the Japanese rate of fire and they had essentially lost the gunnery duel within the first 30 minutes. On the *Orel*, its poorly disciplined crew virtually fell apart after suffering less than 10 percent casualties. During the battle, Russian battleships fired about 900 12-in and 360 10-in rounds – almost triple the number of Japanese heavy shells fired – but significantly fewer 6-in and 8-in rounds. The Russians scored 37 12-in hits, or 4.1 percent, but the rounds suffered from a much higher "dud" rate (33 percent) at Tsushima than at Yellow Sea, probably due to ammunition deterioration incurred on the eight-month voyage from the Baltic. Despite the decision to offload most of the *Shimosa*-filled shells, both *Mikasa* and *Shikishima* suffered premature explosions in one of their 12-in guns, indicating continuing problems with propellant and fuses. However, the rate of fire for main guns was not a determining factor at Tsushima. Togo's battleships fired their main guns at a much lower rate of fire than at Yellow Sea in order to conserve ammunition for an extended battle; the *Mikasa* averaged only one salvo every 7.6 minutes and the *Shikishima* one every 9.6 minutes, while the *Orel* had fired so quickly that by dusk it had only three rounds left for its aft 12-in turret.

During the course of 16 months of naval combat, Japan committed six battleships and lost two, both to mines. Russia committed a total of 15 battleships to the theater of war, of which 12 were sunk (five by siege howitzers, three by naval gunfire, two by torpedoes and two scuttled), two were captured and one was interned. Particularly shocking was the loss of all four *Borodino*-class battleships in their first action, along with the deaths of over 2,600 of their crews.

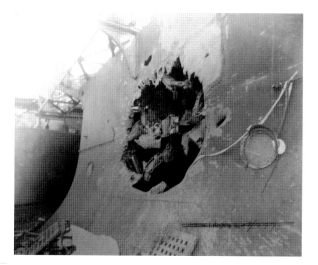

Damage to *Orel*'s port side from another Japanese high explosive shell, which appears to have exploded on contact. (Naval Historical Center, NH66262)

# CONCLUSION

*A shout of victory at Japan Sea is a shout to glorify the empire.*

Japanese poem honoring victory at Tsushima

Both Japan and Russia made technical choices before the war and tactical choices during the war that affected how their battleships performed in combat. Despite the fact that Japan won a crushing victory, it is important to note that both sides made some good choices that panned out and some bad choices that resulted in unnecessary casualties or damage.

The key technical choices involved how to maximize firepower to increase the probability of incapacitating an enemy battleship, how to survive an enemy's bombardment in a gunnery duel and how to build a battleship with the best mix of speed, range and sea-keeping capabilities. The Russian Navy made the conservative decision to rely on large-caliber armor-piercing rounds to sink their enemies, since that was the widely accepted European concept of of naval combat during the 1890s. While aware of new explosives such as Lyddite and Melinite, the Russian Navy preferred the proven gun cotton after early experiments with Melinite resulted in fatal accidents. The Russian Navy played it safe in terms of firepower and thus their battleships went to war with shells that had little chance of penetrating an enemy armor belt or causing significant explosive damage, but which were fairly safe to use. Being the challenger, the Japanese were more inclined to take chances and they bet heavily upon new explosives and propellants to give them the edge in gunnery duels. Instead, *Shimosa* and cordite proved to be highly unstable, bursting gun barrels during sustained firing and then eventually sinking the flagship *Mikasa*. Other navies also went through this dangerous phase with volatile new explosives; the French navy lost the battleships *Iéna* in 1907 and *Liberté* in 1911 to magazine explosions, as did the Royal Navy's *Bulwark* in 1914.

The Japanese also committed themselves fully to incorporating newly developed British rangefinders, telescopic sights and fire-control techniques, but these only gave them an advantage when combat occurred at 6km or less.

Following the British example, the Japanese opted to concentrate their armor protection to cover the central battery, while the Russians emphasized recent French concepts and maximized protection at the waterline and below, to protect against mines and torpedoes. Due to these choices, Japanese battleships stood up better under gunfire, particularly at long range. Russian battleships had better survivability against mines and torpedoes, as demonstrated by the fact that the Japanese lost two of their three battleships that were mined, while the Russians lost only one ship in its four mining incidents. Although the Russians had a design advantage since more of their battleships mounted the better Krupp armor, this did not translate into any real advantage since neither side could effectively penetrate each other's main armor belt at ranges beyond 6km. However, the Japanese switch to high explosive common shells revealed that the lightly protected and inflammable upper works of a battleship were a great place to start a raging bonfire that could rapidly make the ship combat-ineffective. Thus, armor plate only offered one type of protection; removing all the excess boats and ventilator shafts and improving damage-control capabilities represented a more holistic approach.

The Japanese accepted the British broad-beamed, flush-deck hull designs as suited for their purposes: their battleships operated close to home bases so they didn't need to carry a large amount of coal and they didn't have to transit through any canals. Both sides experimented with different types of boilers in order to gain an extra knot or two of speed, and both were saddled with ships equipped with promising but defective machinery such as the Niclausse boilers. Despite emphasizing speed in design, Japanese battleships only had a one- or two-knot advantage over Russian battleships that were not overloaded or damaged. On the other hand, the Russians were forced to build battleships in the Baltic and send them 29,000km to serve in the Pacific, so seaworthiness and the ability to fit through narrow canals drove them toward narrower hulls and greater freeboard, which created stability concerns. The much-criticized tumblehome hull shape adopted by the later Russian battleships was in fact ideal for a ship that had to spend a great deal of time in oceanic transits, although this hull form proved to be dangerously unstable once damage degraded its watertight integrity.

Tactically, the Russian Navy placed its emphasis on a fleet of very powerful battleships for sea control, but neglected to develop lighter units to supplement the battle fleet. At the outset of the war, the Russians had only four armored cruisers in the Pacific and three were at Vladivostok, where their primary mission was commerce raiding. Togo had eight armored cruisers, which were designed to support the battleships and join the battle line as needed. The Japanese decision to use armored cruisers as substitute battleships was a risky choice that they got away with in 1904–05, causing other navies to draw the post-war conclusion that this was an acceptable

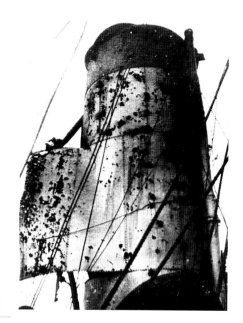

Fragmentation damage to one of the funnels on the battleship *Imperator Nikolai I* at Tsushima. (Naval Historical Center, NH84762)

tactical option. Instead, during World War I, British and German armored cruisers that tried to go toe-to-toe with battleships were quickly blasted to pieces. Cost constraints forced Togo to go to war with fewer battleships than his opponent, but a more balanced fleet.

Command and control also proved to be far more difficult in modern naval warfare, despite the advent of radio. Togo had great difficulty coordinating his main battle line with his cruisers and destroyers at Yellow Sea and the actions were spread over such large areas that traditional signal flags were often not visible. The Russians also found that leader casualties on a battleship rapidly reduced combat efficiency and that an incapacitated captain or fleet commander invariably led to chaos.

Finally, the surprising lethality of mines placed enormous constraints upon battleship operations in coastal waters – a lesson that would be relearned in 1915, when the Allies lost two battleships to Turkish mines in the Dardenelles. The Russians laid 4,275 mines during the war, which sank two Japanese battleships, two cruisers, five gunboats and six destroyers, indicating that the Russian naval strategy of attrition caused by defensive mine warfare might well have crippled the resource-poor IJN if the Russian Army could have held Port Arthur. However, the Japanese faith in using offensive torpedo attacks to degrade the Russian battleship fleet was misplaced and the threat of torpedo boat attacks upon battleships proved to be vastly overrated. During the course of the war the Japanese fired over 350 torpedoes but scored only a few hits, mostly on crippled or stationary ships.

Even before the Russo-Japanese War, naval designers had been drifting toward the "all-big-gun" battleship concept, to break away from the standard ship equipped with only four main guns and a vast assortment of smaller-caliber weapons. Twelve days before Tsushima was fought, the Japanese laid down the *Satsuma* at Kure naval yard – not only the first battleship built in Japan, but the first of a new type of battleship. The Japanese had intended to equip the *Satsuma* with 12 12-in guns, but shortages forced them to substitute four 12-in and 12 10-in guns. Five months later, the British began construction of HMS *Dreadnought*, equipped with 10 12-in guns and turbine engines, which set the standard for battleships for the rest of the 20th century. Thanks to efficient British shipyards, HMS *Dreadnought* was completed in December 1906, three-and-a-half years before the *Satsuma* was completed. By 1907, a new generation of armor-piercing capped (APC) rounds with TNT filler were introduced, which substantially changed the tactical lessons of the Russo-Japanese War. Britain, Germany, Japan, Russia and the United States all began building new fleets of improved dreadnoughts to contest naval supremacy in the next series of wars, but with developments in submarines and aircraft evolving rapidly, the battleship's days were numbered.

*Mikasa*, preserved as a memorial since 1961. A statue of Admiral Togo stands in front of his former flagship. (Author's collection)

# FURTHER READING

"The Battle of the Sea of Japan: The Official Version of the Japanese General Staff," translated by Lt W. Y. Hoadley, USMC in United States Naval Institute *Proceedings* Vol. 40 No. 4, July–August 1914.

Balakin, S. A., *Eskadennyy Bronenosets Retvizan*, Moscow, Arsenal Collection, 2005.

Brook, Peter, "Armstrong Battleships Built for Japan," *Warship International* Vol. 22 No. 3, 1985.

Brown, David K., "Technical Lessons of the Russo-Japanese War," in *Warship*, London, Conway Maritime Press, 1996.

Brown, David K., *Warrior to Dreadnought: Warship Development 1860–1905*, London, Chatham Publishing, 1997.

Busch, Noel F., *The Emperor's Sword: Japan vs. Russia in the Battle of Tsushima*, New York, Funk & Wagnalls, 1969.

Campbell, N. J. M., "The Battle of Tsushima," Parts 1–4, *Warship International*, Vol. 2 Nos. 5–8, 1980.

Connaughton, Richard, *Rising Sun and Tumbling Bear*, London, Cassell, 2003.

Corbett, Julian S., *Maritime Operations in the Russo-Japanese War 1904–1905*, Annapolis, MD, United States Naval Institute Press, 1994.

Gardiner, Robert (editor), *Steam, Steel and Shellfire: The Steam Warship 1815–1905*, London, Conway Maritime Press, 1992.

Hodges, Peter, *The Big Gun: Battleship Main*

The battleship *Tsesarevich* after the Battle of the Yellow Sea. Although her funnels have both been badly holed, the ship's armament and propulsion were still intact and the crew had suffered only 8 percent casualties. (Naval Historical Center, NH84783)

The battleship *Oslyabya* – the first modern battleship sunk solely by gunfire. Note the 6-in bow chaser gun mounted just above the Imperial crest. (Naval Historical Center, NH60706)

*Armament 1860–1945*, Annapolis, MD, Naval Institute Press, 1981.

Hough, Richard, *The Fleet that had to Die*, Edinburgh, Birlinn Ltd, 2000.

McCallum, Iain, "The Riddle of the Shell, 1914–18," in *Warship* 2002–2003, London, Conway Maritime Press, 2005.

McLaughlin, Stephen, *Russian & Soviet Battleships*, Annapolis, MD, Naval Institute Press, 2003.

McLaughlin, Stephen, "Aboard Orel at Tsushima" in *Warship* 2005, London, Conway Maritime Press, 2005.

Mitchell, Donald W., *A History of Russian and Soviet Sea Power*, New York, Macmillan Publishing Co., 1974.

Novoy-Pribikov, Aleksei, *Tsushima*, New York, Alfred A. Knopf, 1937.

Pleshakov, Constantine, *The Tsar's Last Armada*, New York, Basic Books, 2002.

Semenoff, Vladimir I., *Rasplata* [The Reckoning], New York, E. P. Dutton, 1909.

Semenoff, Vladimir I., *The Battle of Tsushima*, New York, E. P. Dutton, 1907.

Shirokorad, Aleksandr V., *Entsiklopediia otechestvennoi artillerii* [Encyclopedia of Fatherland (Russian) Artillery], Minsk, Kharvest, 2000.

Warner, Denis and Peggy, *The Tide at Sunrise: A History of the Russo-Japanese War, 1904–1905*, New York, Charterhouse, 1974.

# WEBSITES:

http://rjw.narod.ru [in Russian]

http://www.russojapanesewar.com The Russo-Japanese War Research Society

# INDEX